Reflections in the Light

Daily Thoughts and Affirmations

Revised Edition

SHAKTI GAWAIN

Compiled by Denise Grimshaw

Nataraj Publishing
a division of

NEW WORLD LIBRARY
NOVATO, CALIFORNIA

Nataraj Publishing

a division of

New World Library
14 Pamaron Way
Novato, California 94949

Cover design: Alexandra Graham
Text design and typography: Tona Pearce Myers

Library of Congress Cataloging-in-Publication Data
  Gawain, Shakti
Reflections in the light : daily thoughts and affirmations/Shakti Gawain ;
  compiled by Denise Grimshaw. — Rev. ed.
  p. cm.
"Based in part on Creative visualization . . . and Living in the light" — T.p. verso.
Includes index.
ISBN 978-1-57731-410-3
  1. Self-actualization (Psychology) 2. Conduct of life. 3. Affirmations.
I. Grimshaw, Denise. II. Title.
BF637.S4G393 2003
158.1'28—dc21   2003043007

First printing, May 2003
ISBN 978-1-57731-410-3
Printed in Canada on acid-free, partially recycled paper

10 9 8 7 6 5

Introduction

The purpose of this book is to give readers an inspirational message, a useful tool, or just some interesting food for thought each day. We hope it will serve to trigger your own thoughts, reactions, and creative ideas.

Most of the material in *Reflections in the Light* has been excerpted from my books *Creative Visualization* and *Living in the Light*. In many cases the quotes are verbatim from those books; in most cases they have been edited or revised slightly to stand on their own as daily entries; a few are newly written for this book.

Those of you who have already read my previous books will find this book a handy way to review and remind yourself of familiar concepts and techniques. For those readers who have not read the other books, we have attempted to make each day's entry clear and self-explanatory, but if you have any difficulty understanding the terminology or concepts you may wish to refer to the glossary, or to read the original books in order to gain more clarity.

Each daily entry has a heading, a short message or meditation, and an affirmation. The easiest way to use this book is simply to pick it up and read it at some point each day, and perhaps say the affirmation to yourself a few times throughout the day.

For those who wish to spend a little more time and use this book as a tool for daily study, here is a suggested way to do so. Read the message each morning, think about it (or do the exercise if one is given) and write any responses, feelings, or thoughts that it triggers for you, how it applies to your life, and so on. If you like the affirmation that is given, write it a few times and think of it throughout the day. If you don't care for the affirmation given, write one of your own and use it the same way. In the evening, read it once again and write any further thoughts or experiences you have had in relation to this topic.

There are certain recurring themes throughout the book. In some cases a particular topic may be continued for several days or even a whole month (for example, the month of March is devoted to creative visualization). In other cases, a topic may be introduced for only a day or two and then reappear frequently in later months. In this way, we hope to provide both continuity and variety over the course of a year, no matter what date you begin using the book.

All of us who have worked on this book extend our loving thoughts to you and hope that you find it a useful companion on your journey of self-development.

— Shakti Gawain

Acknowledgments

I would like to thank Denise Grimshaw for her insight and creativity and for the many hours of research it took to collect all the diverse quotes and compile them into a form that works as a daily meditation over the course of a year.

Special thanks as well to Kathleen Holland for her many helpful suggestions, creative contributions, and hard work editing and organizing the manuscript.

Thanks, too, to Kathryn Altman for coordinating the project, to Marc Allen for his support and encouragement, to Carol LaRusso and Katherine Dieter for their editing and overall help, and to Elizabeth Preim for her assistance in organizing the original manuscript.

For the second edition I'd like to thank Georgia Hughes, Tona Pearce Myers, and the rest of the team at New World Library.

Reflections in the Light

Winter

January 1

Creating a new way of life

We are living in a very exciting and powerful time. On the deepest level of consciousness, a radical spiritual transformation is taking place. On a worldwide level, we are being challenged to let go of our present way of life and create an entirely new one. We are, in fact, in the process of releasing our old world and building a new world in its place.

The change begins with each individual, but as more and more individuals are being transformed, the mass consciousness is increasingly affected, and the results will be manifested in the world around us.

Each day I am creating my life anew.

January 2

As the new emerges, the old gives way

For many people, this time may be distressing because the world situation and/or our personal lives may seem to be going from bad to worse. It's as if many things that used to work are not working anymore.

Painful though it may be at times, these changes are part of a "healing crisis" taking place in our world. The simple truth is that the old way of life never brought us the deep fulfillment, satisfaction, and joy that we have always sought. We must let go of the old forms which limit us or don't fit anymore in order to make way for the new.

I release the old and make way for the new.

January 3

Looking within

The old world was based on external focus. We had come to believe that the material world was the only reality. Thus, feeling essentially lost, empty, and alone, we have continually attempted to find happiness through addiction to external things such as money, material possessions, relationships, work, fame, food, and drugs.

Today, as we begin to remember our fundamental spiritual connection, we can look within for the source of our satisfaction, joy, and fulfillment.

I find my spiritual connection within.

January 4

Return to kindergarten

Our first task in building the new world is to admit that our "life education" has not necessarily taught us a satisfying way to live. We suffer from a vague sense that there must be something more, some deeper meaning. We must "return to kindergarten" and start to learn a way of life that is contrary to the way we approached things before — a way of life based on trust of our own inner truth.

I am learning a new way of life.

The creative power within

The new world is being built as we open to the higher power of the universe and consciously allow that creative energy to move through us. As each of us connects with our spiritual awareness, we learn that the creative power of the universe is within us. We also learn that we can create our own reality and take responsibility for doing so.

The creative power of the universe is now flowing through me.

January 6

Create your life the way you want it

Many of us have had the attitude that life is something that happens to us and that all we can do is make the best of it. It is basically a victim's position, giving power to people and things outside of ourselves. We are beginning to realize that the power rests in us, that we can choose to create our life the way we want it to be.

I am now creating my life the way I want it to be.

January 7

A prosperous world

There is more than enough to go around for every being on earth if we are willing to open our minds to that possibility and change our ways of using the world's resources.

We can all be naturally prosperous, in a way that is balanced and harmonious with one another and with the earth that nourishes us.

I am creating balanced, harmonious prosperity in my life.

January 8

Open your eyes to goodness, beauty,
and abundance

Imagine yourself as a successful, satisfied, prosperous, fulfilled person. Really open your eyes to the goodness, beauty, and abundance that are all around you. Imagine this world transformed into a healthy and prosperous environment in which everyone can flourish.

Today I am fulfilled, successful, and prosperous.

January 9

Emptiness is filled from the inside

When we are most unhappy, we have a starved feeling in some way. We feel that life in general and other people in particular are not giving us what we need. We try desperately to grasp the love and satisfaction that we crave from the outside. Yet we are actually choking off the supply.

The new world is based on trust of the universe within us. We recognize that the creative intelligence and energy of the universe is the fundamental source of everything. Once we connect with this and surrender to it, everything is ours. Emptiness is filled from the inside.

I am being filled from the source within me.

Our guiding force

Once we acknowledge the higher power of the universe, the obvious question arises — "How can we contact this power, or gain access to it?" The knowingness that resides in each of us can be accessed through what we call our intuition. By learning to contact, listen to, and act on our intuition, we can directly connect to the higher power of the universe and allow it to become our guiding force.

The higher power of the universe is guiding my life through my intuition.

January 11

The intuitive mind

The intuitive mind has access to an infinite supply of information. It is able to tap into a deep storehouse of knowledge and wisdom — the universal mind. It is also able to sort out this information and supply us with exactly what we need, when we need it. Our role is to listen to our intuition, trust its guidance, and learn to act on it step-by-step in our lives.

I trust my intuitive guidance.

January 12

A wise being lives inside of you

There is a wise being living inside of you. It is your intuitive self. Focus your awareness into a deep place in your body, a place where your "gut feelings" reside. You can communicate with it by silently talking to it, making requests, or asking questions. Then relax, don't think too hard with your mind, and be open to receiving answers. These messages are usually very simple, relate to the present moment, not to the past or future, and they feel right.

I trust the wisdom inside of me.

January 13

Step-by-step, we are shown the way

Though the message of the intuitive self may come through a bit at a time, if we learn to follow the supply of information piece by piece, the necessary course of action will unfold. As we learn to rely on this guidance, life takes on a flowing, effortless quality. Our life, feelings, and actions interweave harmoniously with those of others around us.

Moment by moment, I'm learning to trust the flow of my life.

January 14

Trust your feelings and act on them

Trust the deepest feelings that you get and act on them. If they are truly from your intuition, you will find that they lead to a feeling of greater aliveness and power and more opportunities begin to open up. If you don't feel more alive and empowered, you may not have been truly acting from your intuition, but from some other voice in you. With practice, you will discover that your intuitive sense has an energy that is different from your other thoughts and feelings, and you will learn to recognize it.

As I trust my intuitive feelings and act on them, I feel powerful and alive.

January 15

Freedom from struggle

We strive so hard to make our lives the way we want them to be. As you begin this day, imagine that you can give up struggling for a whole day. Relax for a while, and trust that your needs will be met by the natural flow of life.

The philosophy of *being here now* and letting go of attachment is a very freeing experience. When you do this, you discover that you're really perfectly okay; in fact you feel quite wonderful. You can just let yourself be, let the world be, and give up to the struggle of trying to change things.

I relax and let myself be.

January 16

Change

Change happens not by trying to *make* yourself change, but by being conscious of what's *not* working. You can then ask your higher self for help in releasing the old and bringing in the new pattern. Remember, the darkest hour is just before the dawn — change often occurs just when you've given up, or when you least expect it.

I am open and willing to change.

Follow your creative energy

To whatever degree you listen to and follow your intuition, you will become a creative channel for the higher power of the universe. When you willingly follow where your creative energy leads, the higher power can come through you to manifest its creative work. When this happens, you will find yourself flowing with the energy, doing what you really want to do, and feeling the power of the universe moving through you.

As I follow my intuition,
creative energy flows through me.

January 18

You are a channel for creativity

In using the word "channel," I am not referring to the psychic process of trance channeling. By channeling I mean being in touch with and bringing through the wisdom and creativity of your own deepest source. To be a channel is to be fully and freely yourself, consciously aware that you are a vehicle for the creativity of the universe.

I am a channel for the creative power of the universe.

Higher purpose

We each have a significant contribution to make in this lifetime. I call this contribution our higher purpose. It always involves being yourself totally, completely, and naturally, and doing something or many things that you genuinely love to do, that come easily to you. As you learn to follow your feelings, dreams, and visions, to explore doing things you love, you begin to discover your higher purpose.

Every moment is a moment of creation and each moment of creation contains infinite possibilities.

By being myself and doing what I love, I make a significant contribution to life.

January 20

Fulfillment is found in daily life

Fulfillment comes from what you are doing at this very moment. It is not a matter of doing things now for gratification later. (I will work now so I can get a better job later. I will work hard now, so that I can retire and enjoy life. I will work hard now to have enough money for a vacation.) It is the fulfillment of what you are doing now that counts. Even the simplest things are significant.

I find fulfillment in everything I do.

January 21

Being, doing, and having

We can think of life having three dimensions: being, doing, and having. Often we attempt to live our lives backwards. We try to *have* more money in order to feel we can *do* more of what we want, so we can *be* happier. The way it actually works is the reverse. We must first *be* who we really are, then *do* what we feel guided to do, in order to *have* what we *want*.

I allow myself to be;
I do what feels right;
I have everything I truly want.

January 22

Letting go

Let us imagine that life is a river. Most people are clinging to the bank, afraid to let go, and risk being carried along by the current of the river. When the pain of hanging on becomes greater than the fear of letting go, we let go and the river begins to carry us along safely. Once we are used to being in the flow of the river, we can begin to look ahead and guide our course. We choose which of the many branches of the river we prefer to follow, all the while still going with the flow. We can enjoy being here now, flowing with what is and at the same time, guide ourselves consciously toward our goals by taking full responsibility for creating our own lives.

As I relax and let go, I flow toward my greatest good.

The search for fulfillment

At this time, many human beings (and other species as well) on the earth are still struggling for physical survival. Yet there are an increasing number of us who no longer have to be preoccupied primarily with sheer survival. We have the opportunity, and thus the responsibility, to begin looking for deeper fulfillment on spiritual, mental, and emotional levels. We are searching for greater meaning and purpose in our lives, and for ways to live more responsibly and harmoniously on our planet.

I am finding meaning, purpose, and fulfillment in my life.

January 24

Spirit and form

Spirit is the essence of consciousness, the energy of the universe that creates all things. Each one of us is a part of that spirit — a divine entity. So the spirit is the higher self, the eternal being that lives within us.

Form is the physical world: body, mind, personality. We as spiritual beings created the physical world as a place to learn. We're here to learn how to master the process of creation — to learn how to consciously channel the creative energy of spirit into physical form.

I am learning to create form from spirit.

January 25

What is creative visualization?

Creative visualization is the technique of using your imagination to create what you want in your life. You are already using it every day, every minute in fact. It is your natural power of imagination, the basic creative energy of the universe which you use constantly whether or not you are aware of it. All you have to do is relax deeply and picture a desired goal in your mind exactly the way you want it to be.

I am now visualizing my life exactly the way I want it.

Contacting the source

One of the most important steps in making creative visualization work is to have the experience of connecting with your inner creative source. I like to think of contacting the source as connecting with your higher self, the godlike being who dwells within you. Being in contact with your higher self is characterized by a deep sense of knowingness. You know that you are creating your own world and that you have infinite power to create it as you desire.

I am in contact with my source and am creating my life as I desire it to be.

January 27

Our divine potential

There is no separation between God and us. We are expressions of the creative principle on this level of existence. We contain the potential for everything within us. Manifestation through creative visualization is the process of realizing and making visible on the physical plane our divine potential.

I am expressing more and more of my potential.

January 28

Have fun with it

Get comfortable. Relax your body. Breathe deeply and slowly. Start to imagine something you want, exactly as you would like it. Have fun with it. Pretend you are a child daydreaming about what you want for your birthday. Really let yourself imagine how good it would feel to have what you want. End your visualization with a statement to yourself. "This or something better now manifests for me in totally satisfying and harmonious ways for the highest good of all concerned."

I have fun visualizing what I want.

January 29

A source deep within

As we explore the process of creating our own reality, we begin to realize that the creative power we are feeling is coming from some source other than our personality. It seems to come from some place deep within ourselves. We become interested in discovering what this creative force is and how it works. We realize the "it" (our higher self) knows more than "I" (our personality self). We find out what the inner guidance is telling us and follow it.

I feel creative power coming from deep within me.

Your own personal sanctuary

Close your eyes, relax your body, imagine yourself in a beautiful, natural environment — somewhere you feel comfortable, relaxed, and peaceful. Explore your environment, noticing details, sounds, and smells. Do anything you would like to make the place more homelike and comfortable. Build a house or shelter or just surround the whole area with a golden light of protection and safety. From now on this is your own personal inner sanctuary. You will always find it healing and relaxing. It is a place of special power.

Within me is a special place of
serenity and power.

January 31

Release the old, receive the new

Sit or lie down, relax, close your eyes, and take a few deep breaths. As you exhale, imagine that you are letting go of everything you don't want or need. Imagine that your old patterns and limitations are gently dissolving. As you exhale and release the old, you create space for something new. As you inhale, you breathe in life energy. Imagine a new way of life opening up, filled with aliveness and vitality.

With every breath,
I release the old and receive the new.

February 1

There is a higher intelligence

The foundation for life in the new world we are creating is built on the understanding that there is a higher intelligence, a fundamental creative power or energy in the universe which is the substance of all that exists.

Many terms are used to express an experience of this power. Although it is difficult to convey with words and rational concepts, each of us has at some time felt a sense of oneness, knowingness, and unity with the divine presence.

I feel the presence of a power greater than myself.

February 2

A presence within us

As we surrender to the power of the universe and trust it more, we find our relationship with this higher essence becoming more personal. We can literally feel a presence within us, guiding us, loving us, teaching us, encouraging us. The universe can be teacher, guide, friend, mother, father, lover, creative genius, fairy godmother, even Santa Claus. In other words, whatever we feel we need or want can be fulfilled through this inner connection.

I have a personal relationship with a higher power.

February 3

Distinguishing intuition

Your intuition is always one hundred percent correct, but it takes time to hear it correctly. If you are willing to risk acting on what you believe to be true and risk making mistakes, you will learn very fast by paying attention to what works and what doesn't work. The first step is to pay more attention to what you feel inside, to the dialogue that goes on within you. Through practice you will be able to distinguish your intuitive voice from other thoughts and voices.

*I am hearing my intuition
more clearly every day.*

February 4

Observe your inner dialogue

Anyone who has practiced meditation knows how difficult it can be to quiet our "mind talk" in order to connect with our deeper, wise, intuitive mind. One traditional meditation practice is to simply observe the inner dialogue as objectively as possible. This is a valuable experience that allows you to become aware of the types of thoughts you habitually think. Many of these thoughts come from programming we picked up long ago, which is still influencing us. Once we recognize these thought patterns, we can begin to change old habits. We can tell the difference between the limiting, habitual, mind talk and the voice of our inner guidance.

I pay attention to the thoughts I think.

February 5

A natural human experience

When we speak of following your inner voice, remember that most people do not experience it as a voice. Often it's more like a feeling, an energy, a sense of "This feels right," or "This doesn't feel right." It's a simple, natural, human experience that we have lost touch with and need to reclaim.

I reclaim my natural ability to follow my intuition.

February 6

Intuition meditation

Get in a comfortable position, sitting or lying down. Close your eyes and relax. Take several deep, slow, long breaths and as you exhale each time, imagine relaxing your body and relaxing your mind. Then imagine moving your awareness into a very deep place inside of you — deep in your solar plexus or your belly. Keep going deeper until you find a quiet resting place inside. Imagine that in that deep place you contact your own inner truth. Ask if there is a message for you or something you need to know or remember. Or ask a specific question. Then relax and feel or "listen" to what comes to you. It may be a thought, a feeling, or an image. Just receive whatever comes. Don't try to figure it out with your mind or you will block the process. If it seems like nothing happens, don't worry about it. Practice this regularly in a relaxed way, and you will begin to feel in touch with your intuition.

I am in touch with my intuitive feelings.

February 7

Practice listening

It takes practice to hear and trust your intuition. The more you do it, the easier it will become. Eventually you will be in touch with your intuitive feelings much of the time. Ask yourself questions. Know that the wise being within you, an incredible source of power and strength, is available to answer your questions and guide you. As you grow sensitive to this guidance from the intuitive feelings from within, you will gain a sense of knowing what you need to do in any situation.

I trust my inner knowing in all situations.

February 8

Just be yourself

It isn't necessary to be perfect to be a channel for the universe. You just have to be real. Be yourself. The more honest and spontaneous you are, the more freely the creative force can flow through you. As it does, it cleans out the remnants of old blockages. The more you are true to yourself, the clearer your channel gets.

Today I am honest, spontaneous, and true to myself.

February 9

We are all geniuses

We are all geniuses, each in our own unique way. We discover the nature of our particular genius when we stop trying to conform to our own or other people's models, and learn to be ourselves, allowing our natural channel to open. Then we discover that we each have something special to offer the world that no one else can duplicate.

In my own unique way,
I am a genius.

Every creative genius has been a channel

*E*very creative genius has been a channel for the divine power of the universe. Every master work has been created through the channeling process. Great works are not created by the personality alone. They arise from a deep inspiration on the universal level, and are then expressed and brought into form through the individual personality.

*I am a channel
for creative inspiration.*

February 11

We each have unique gifts

In creating our new world, things may come together in unexpected ways and fascinating combinations. Perhaps you haven't found your career because it doesn't exist yet. Your particular and unique way of expressing yourself has never existed before and will never be repeated again.

I am discovering my own unique expression.

Experiencing our feelings

When we have suppressed and closed off our feelings, we cannot contact the universe within us. We cannot hear our intuitive voice, and we certainly can't enjoy being alive. When we are willing to fully experience a particular feeling such as fear, anger, loneliness, or confusion and embrace that emotion without judgment, the blocked energy releases quickly and the feeling dissolves, allowing us to feel more peaceful and open.

*I accept and experience
all my feelings.*

February 13

Rainbow colors of life

There are no such things as negative or positive feelings. We make them negative or positive by our rejection or acceptance of them. All feelings are part of the wonderful, ever changing sensation of being alive. If we accept all the different feelings, they become so many rainbow colors of life.

All my feelings are a natural
expression of life.

February 14

Falling in love with ourselves

When we fall in love with someone, we are also falling in love with aspects of ourselves that we see reflected in that person. We may feel that our loved one has qualities that we don't have, but those qualities exist in us too and are as yet undiscovered or undeveloped.

Today, think of each person you love and imagine him or her as a mirror, reflecting your own beauty and lovability. The more you can love yourself through these reflections, the more you can truly love and appreciate others.

I am falling in love
with myself.

February 15

We can have everything

As long as we focus on the outer world, there will always be an empty, hungry, lost place inside us that needs to be filled. When we keep our focus on the universe inside, we can have everything external — money, success, and fulfilling relationships — as well as that incredible connection inside ourselves.

I am receiving everything from the source within me.

February 16

Feeling more alive

*E*ach time that we choose to trust and follow our intuition our channel opens more. More of the life force flows through. The cells of our bodies actually receive more energy, renewing and revitalizing themselves faster. Physically, emotionally, and mentally we feel more alive. More of our spirit can shine through. Our body stays healthy and beautiful, and radiates vitality.

I feel the life force flowing through my body.

February 17

Surrender to life

A part of us wants life, wants to make the commitment to live as fully as possible, and is willing to trust our intuition and follow it from moment to moment. There is another part of us that doesn't trust this inclination. "I can't do this, it's too much, too intense. I don't want to surrender." When we resist the life force, we experience only effort and struggle. When we surrender to life the flow of energy increases, and we feel the passion of being alive.

I surrender to life.

February 18

The moment of total surrender

When we finally give up the struggle to find fulfill-ment outside of ourselves, we have nowhere to go but within. It is at this moment of total surrender that the light begins to dawn. We expect to hit bottom, but instead we fall through a trapdoor into a bright new world. We rediscover the world of our spirit.

Through surrender,
I find the light within me.

February 19

Asking for guidance

$\mathcal{I}$f you have a problem that you need help with, try this technique. Sit or lie down in a comfortable position, close your eyes, take a few deep breaths, and relax deeply. Imagine that you are in touch with your deepest inner wisdom. Formulate the problem in your mind, and ask for guidance from that inner source. Relax for a few minutes and be receptive to any feelings, images, or thoughts that come to you. The guidance may come to you right away, or it may come sometime within the next few hours or days.

I am asking for and listening to my inner guidance.

February 20

Take a moment

One important step in learning to hear and follow your intuition is to simply practice checking in regularly, at least twice a day, more often if possible. Take a moment or two to relax and listen to your gut feelings. Cultivate this habit of communicating with your inner self. Ask for help and guidance when you need it and practice listening for answers.

I listen to my gut feelings.

February 21

It takes practice

We need to reeducate ourselves to listen to and trust the inner truths that come to us through our intuitive feelings. We must learn to act on them, even though it may feel risky and frightening at first, because we are no longer playing it safe, doing what we "should" do, pleasing others, following rules, or deferring to outside authority.

Learning to trust our intuition is an art form, and like all other art forms, it takes practice to perfect. We have to be willing to make "mistakes," to try something and fail, and then try something different the next time. If we hold back out of fear of being wrong, learning to trust our intuition could take a lifetime.

I am learning to trust my intuition.

February 22

Don't push yourself!

You can't always force yourself to follow your intuitive feelings. Sometimes it simply feels too difficult or scary. Don't push past what you are ready to do. Simply observe the process and be honest with yourself about how it feels and what happens. If you love and accept yourself exactly as you are, change will happen naturally and spontaneously.

Today I love myself and accept myself exactly as I am.

February 23

Each of us plays a unique instrument

We each play a unique instrument in the orchestra of life. If we play our part without regard for the conductor's direction or the rest of the orchestra, then we have total chaos. If we try to take our cues only from those around us, it will be impossible to achieve harmony. However, if we watch the conductor (our intuition) and follow its direction, we can experience the joy of playing our unique part, and at the same time experience ourselves as part of a greater harmonious whole.

I am a unique and special instrument.

We receive the support we need

If we are honest with ourselves, we will readily admit that we are not making great music on the guidance of our rational mind alone. By tuning into our intuition and allowing it to become the guiding force in our lives, we allow the conductor to take his rightful place as leader of the orchestra. Rather than losing our individual freedom, we receive the support we need to express our individuality.

In harmony with the whole,
I find my individual freedom.

February 25

Learning from our mistakes

We must remember that we are babies in the new world. We learn by making lots of mistakes and often we may feel ignorant, frightened, or unsure of ourselves. But we would not get angry at a baby every time he fell down, so we must try not to criticize ourselves for our natural learning process.

I learn from all my mistakes.

Developing all levels

We are now learning to live more fully in accordance with the laws of the universe. We are challenged to explore all aspects of our human experience and to develop all levels of our being — the spiritual, mental, and emotional as well as the physical.

As we do this work, we experience an increasing sense of wholeness, empowerment, aliveness, and a feeling of being "on purpose" in our lives.

I am developing all levels of my being — spiritual, mental, emotional, and physical.

February 27

Never alone

When you find a deep connection with yourself, you will seldom feel truly alone anymore. In fact, it is in physical aloneness that you will often find the most powerful communion with the higher power. At such times, the previously empty places inside of you are filled with the life force. Here you will find a constant guiding presence that tells you which move to make next, and helps you to learn the lesson that lies in taking each step along your path.

*I love being alone
with the higher power.*

February 28

Becoming a channel for the universe

To become a clear channel for the universe presents the highest challenge and offers the greatest potential fulfillment for every human being. Being a channel means living fully and passionately in the world, having deep relationships, playing, working, creating, enjoying money and material possessions, being yourself, feeling a profound connection with the power of the universe within you, learning and growing from every experience that you have. Then you can watch the universe create through you. It can use you to do its work.

I am living fully and passionately as a clear channel.

February 29

You are like a golden sun

Sit or lie in a comfortable position. Let your body relax completely. Breathe deeply and slowly. Visualize a light within your heart — glowing, radiant, and warm. Feel it spreading and growing, shining out from you further and further until you are like a golden sun radiating loving energy on everything and everyone around you. Say to yourself, "Divine light and divine love are flowing through me and radiating from me to everything around me." Repeat this over and over until you have a strong sense of your own spiritual energy.

Divine light and divine love are flowing through me.

March 1

Creative visualization is magic

Creative visualization is magic in the truest and highest meaning of the word. It involves understanding and aligning yourself with the natural principles that govern the workings of the universe and learning to use these principles in the most conscious and creative way.

I feel the magic of the universe operating in my life.

March 2

"As you sow, so shall you reap"

Consciously having an idea or thought, and holding it in your mind is a process which will tend to attract and create that form on the material plane. "As you sow, so shall you reap." What this means is that we often attract into our lives whatever we think about most, believe in most strongly, accept on the deepest level, and imagine most vividly.

Today I am attracting beauty, joy, and abundance into my life.

March 3

Use creative visualization consciously

In the past, many of us have used our power of creative visualization in a relatively unconscious way. Because of our own deep-seated negative concepts about life, we have automatically and unconsciously expected and imagined lack, limitation, difficulties, and problems to be our lot in life. To one degree or another, we have created these difficulties for ourselves.

Now we have the opportunity to use the conscious power of our minds to create self-love, abundance, freedom, and fulfillment in our lives.

Today I expect the best.

March 4

Everything is energy

Everything in the physical world is made of energy, all vibrating at different rates of speed. Thought is a relatively fine, light form of energy and is quick and easy to change. Matter is relatively dense and compact energy, slower to move and change. All these energy fields are interconnected, so how we think and feel is constantly affecting and being affected by everything around us. We are all part of one great energy system.

I feel at one with the energy of the universe.

March 5

We create first in thought form

When we create something, we always create it first in thought form. An artist first has an idea or inspiration, then creates a painting. The idea is like a blueprint. It creates an image of the form, which then magnetizes and guides the physical energy to flow into that form and eventually manifests on the physical plane.

My thoughts are creating a wonderful blueprint for my life.

March 6

Imagination is the ability to create

The use of creative visualization gives us a key to tap into the natural goodness and bounty of life. Imagination is the ability to create an idea or mental picture in your mind. In creative visualization you use your imagination to create a clear image, sense, or feeling of something you wish to manifest.

My imagination is a powerful tool for creation.

March 7

Relax deeply

It is important to relax deeply when we are first learning to use creative visualization. When our minds and bodies are deeply relaxed and centered, our brain waves change and become slower. As we are able to silence our habitual mind chatter, we have a chance to listen on a deeper level. We become receptive and open to our creative imagination and intuition.

*I am deeply relaxed
and centered.*

March 8

A basic creative visualization exercise

Think of something you desire to have, to do, or to experience. For this exercise, pick something simple and fairly realistic for you.

Sit or lie down in a comfortable position. Take a few long, slow, deep breaths and relax your body and mind. Now imagine yourself doing, having, or experiencing whatever it is that you want. Imagine it as if it is already happening, as if it is true, now. You might see a mental picture of it, or just get a feeling or a sense of what it would be like for you if this wish came true. Let yourself enjoy the experience.

When you feel complete, open your eyes. Know that in visualizing or imagining your goal as if it were already true, you have opened the door to creating it. Repeat this exercise whenever you want to.

This or something better
is now coming true.

Visualizing your goal

Bring your idea or mental picture to mind often, both in quiet meditation periods and also casually throughout the day when you happen to think about it. This way it becomes an integrated part of your life. It becomes more a reality for you and you project it more successfully. Focus on it clearly, yet in a light, gentle way. It is important not to feel like you're working too hard for it, or putting excessive amounts of energy into it. That would hinder rather than help.

I focus on my goals in a gentle, relaxed way.

March 10

To affirm means to make firm

An affirmation is a strong, positive statement that something is already so. It is a way of making firm that which you are imagining. While you are using affirmations, try to temporarily suspend any doubts or disbelief you may have, at least for the moment. Practice getting the feeling that that which you desire is very real and possible.

What I desire is possible.

March 11

Finding the right affirmation

Always choose affirmations that feel totally right for you. What works for one person may not work at all for another. An affirmation should feel positive, expansive, freeing, and/or supportive. If it doesn't, find another one or try changing the words until it feels right. A powerful, effective affirmation may bring up some resistance from the part of you that fears change, but that will dissolve as you work with it. Choose affirmations that feel supportive, freeing, and expansive.

I am now discovering the most powerful affirmations for me.

March 12

Affirmations from the heart

In general, the shorter and simpler the affirmation, the more effective. An affirmation should be a clear statement that conveys a strong feeling. The more feeling it conveys, the stronger impression it makes on your mind. Affirmations that are long, wordy, and theoretical lose their emotional impact. Choose affirmations that come from your heart, not your head.

*As I listen to my heart,
the right affirmation comes to me.*

March 13

Resistance to change

You may feel emotional resistance to any affirmation when you first use it, especially one which is really powerful for you and is going to make a real change in your consciousness. That is simply our initial resistance to change and growth. If doubts or contradicting thoughts arise, don't resist them or try to prevent them. This will tend to give them a power they don't otherwise have. Just let your doubts flow through your consciousness and then return to your positive statements and images.

I accept my resistance and move forward.

March 14

A daily endeavor

If possible, use creative visualization and affirmations a little each day, even if only for five minutes. It is especially good to do creative visualization at night just before sleeping or in the morning just after awakening, because at those times the mind and body often are already deeply relaxed and receptive. A short period of meditation and creative visualization done at midday will relax and renew you and will cause your day to flow more smoothly.

I am now using creative visualization every day.

March 15

Creative visualization —
receptive and active

There are two aspects to creative visualization — receptive and active. In the receptive mode we ask questions and receive answers or guidance from our intuitive mind through words, mental images, or feelings. In the active mode we choose mental images and affirmations and use them as tools to consciously create our reality. Both aspects are important parts of the creative process.

I am developing the receptive and active aspects of my imagination.

March 16

Goals give us direction

*E*very time you have a desire, in a certain sense you have a goal, something you would like to be, do, or have. Some desires are merely passing fancies, but others stay with us and go deeper. Our desires and our goals give us direction and focus. They help point us down our path of action in life.

My desires and goals give me positive direction in life.

March 17

Creating on many levels

Your goal may be on any level — physical, mental, or spiritual. You might imagine yourself with a new home or a new job, or having a satisfying relationship, or feeling calm and confident. You might picture yourself handling a difficult situation easily or imagine yourself taking a restful vacation. You can work on any level — all will have results.

I am creating positive results on all levels of my life.

Enjoy the entire journey

To enjoy your goals, think of them as signposts, pointing you in a certain direction. They give you a focus and help your energy to get moving. The way you go is up to you; you can get very uptight focusing only on getting to your goal or you can relax and enjoy the entire journey, appreciating every unexpected bend and turn of the road, every new opportunity for learning and feeling.

I am relaxing and enjoying every moment of my journey.

March 19

Dissolving barriers

C reative visualization is a means of unblocking or dissolving the barriers we ourselves have created to the naturally harmonious, abundant, and loving flow of the universe. It is only truly effective when it is used in alignment with our highest goals and purposes for the highest good of all beings.

I am dissolving my barriers and finding my highest good.

Having what we want supports others

Because human nature is basically loving, most of us will not allow ourselves to have what we want so long as we believe that we might be depriving others in order to do so. We have to understand in a deep way that living a fulfilling life contributes to the general state of human happiness and inspires and supports others to create more happiness for themselves.

The more I receive, the more others
are able to receive.

March 21

See yourself receiving

As you focus on your goal, make strong positive affirmations to yourself that it has come, or is now coming to you. Imagine yourself receiving or achieving it. Always phrase affirmations in the present tense, not in the future. Don't say, "I will get a wonderful new job," but rather "I now have a wonderful new job." This is not lying to yourself, but acknowledging the fact that everything is created first on the mental plane before it can manifest in objective reality. It is also a way of changing the patterns of how we usually talk to ourselves.

I am achieving my goals easily.

March 22

Every moment is an opportunity

Remember that you are always creating your life new and fresh. You are not trying to redo or change what already exists. To do so would be to resist what is, which creates struggle and conflict. Take the attitude that you are accepting and handling whatever exists in your life while at the same time recognizing that every moment is a new opportunity to begin creating exactly what you desire and will make you the happiest.

*I create my life
anew each day.*

March 23

Desire, belief, and acceptance

Creative visualization will work successfully for you if you have the *desire* for, belief in, and acceptance of your goal. You must have a strong and true desire to have or create that which you have chosen. The more you *believe* in your chosen goal, the more able you will be to create it. And you must be willing to *accept* and have that which you are seeking. Together these three elements form a clear intention to manifest your dream.

*I desire, believe in,
and accept my highest good.*

March 24

With perseverance you will succeed

Don't feel discouraged if you don't immediately feel totally successful with your creative visualization. Remember that most of us have had years of negative thought patterns to overcome, so be patient. It has taken a lifetime to create your world the way it is. It may not necessarily change instantly, although it sometimes does. With perseverance you will succeed in creating what seem like many miracles in your life.

In my own time and my own way,
I am creating miracles in my life.

Flow with the moment

Continue to work on the process of affirmation and visualization until you achieve your goal, or no longer have the desire to do so. If you lose interest it may mean that it is time for a new look at what you want. If you find that a goal has changed for you, be sure to acknowledge that to yourself. This helps you avoid getting confused or feeling like you've failed, when you have simply changed. Be willing to flow with the moment. It is easier to be clear about your desire, if you are willing to change as your life changes around you.

As the flow of life changes, I change.

The highest good for all

Creative visualization cannot be used to control the behavior of others or cause them to do something against their will. Its effect is to dissolve our internal barriers to natural harmony and self-realization, allowing everybody to manifest in their most positive way.

As I manifest my own highest good,
I allow others to manifest theirs.

March 27

Writing your goals

Write your most important goals for the next month, six months, year, and/or five years. Write each one in the form of an affirmation, that is, write it in a sentence, in the present tense, as if it had already come true. So, instead of saying, "I want to live in a bigger, sunnier, more beautiful apartment," phrase it this way — "I am now living in a big, sunny, beautiful apartment that I love." This will make it a powerful process of creative visualization.

I am achieving my goals easily, effortlessly, and harmoniously.

March 28

Do something wonderful for yourself

When you achieve a goal, be sure to acknowledge consciously to yourself that it has been completed. Often we achieve things which we have been desiring and visualizing, and we forget to even notice that we have succeeded. So give yourself some appreciation. Do something wonderful for yourself and be sure to thank the universe for fulfilling your request.

*I love and appreciate myself
and the universe within me.*

March 29

In the spirit of the Tao

The only effective way to use creative visualization is in the spirit of the Tao — going with the flow. That means that you don't have to struggle to get where you want to go. You simply put out clearly to the universe where you would like to go, and then patiently and harmoniously follow the flow of the river of life until it takes you there or somewhere even better.

*I patiently trust in the power
of the universe.*

March 30

Pink bubble

Relax, sit or lie down comfortably, close your eyes, and breathe deeply. Imagine something you would like to manifest. Imagine that it has already happened. Picture it, sense it, feel it. Now, surround your fantasy with a pink bubble. Put your goal inside the bubble. Pink is the color associated with the heart, and if this color vibration surrounds whatever you visualize, it will bring to you only that which is in perfect affinity with your being. Now, let go of the bubble and imagine it floating off into the universe. Release it, knowing the universe will bring this (or something better) to you at the right time.

My heart's desire
is coming true.

March 31

You are the constant creator of your life

As you develop the habit of using creative visualization and begin to trust the results it can bring to you, you will find it becomes a state of consciousness in which you know that you are the constant creator of your life. That is the ultimate point of creative visualization: to make every moment of our lives a moment of wondrous creation in which we are just naturally choosing the best, the most beautiful, the most fulfilling lives we can imagine.

My life is
my wondrous creation.

Spring

April 1

The fool

The archetype of the fool can connect us with a very important aspect of ourselves. It is the image of the innocent, childlike person who is not caught in the concepts and stereotypes of the rational, sophisticated mind and therefore is free to perceive and experience life directly as it really is, in the moment.

For today, let go of your adult sophistication and allow yourself to experience the simple delight of a very young child. Be the fool, who, having no complex concepts of how things *should* be, simply enjoys life as it is.

I am filled with innocent delight.

April 2

Our female aspect

The female aspect of our being is our intuitive self. This is the deepest, wisest part of ourselves and is the feminine energy in both men and women. It is the receptive aspect, the open door through which the higher intelligence of the universe can flow, the receiving end of the channel. Our female self communicates to us through our intuition. Those inner promptings, gut feelings, or images come from a deep place within us.

*I listen to and honor
my inner female.*

April 3

Our male aspect

The male aspect of ourselves is action. It is our ability to do things in the physical world — to think, to speak, to move our bodies. Whether you are a man or a woman, your masculine energy enables you to act. It is the outflowing end of the channel. The feminine receives the universal creative energy and the masculine expresses it in the world through action. Thus we have the creative process.

I honor and express my inner male.

April 4

Active and receptive

There two basic ways of getting what we want in life. The masculine, active mode is to go after what you want or *make* it happen. The feminine, receptive mode is to attract to you that which you desire, or *allow* it to happen. Most of us are more comfortable with one or the other of these ways. Whether you are a man or woman, to be fully succesful you need to develop both the active and receptive energies.

I am developing both my active and receptive energies.

April 5

Following our natural rhythm

There is a natural rhythm to the active and receptive energies within us. At times our energy is strong and outgoing — it is time to pursue our goals, take risks, get things accomplished. At other times, our energy is quiet and sensitive, and we need to take time to nurture ourselves, relax, and just "be" for a while. As we trust and follow this rhythm, we attract everything we need and create everything we truly desire.

I am following the natural rhythm of my energy.

April 6

Heal your feelings

In the process of learning to trust your intuition, many old feelings and deep emotional patterns will come to the surface to be healed and released. Feelings of sadness, fear, pain, guilt, and anger may come up. Allow yourself to consciously experience and accept these feelings; as you do so they will naturally begin to release and heal. As the light of awareness penetrates every cell of your body, it dispels the darkness.

As I allow myself to feel my feelings,
I heal them.

Replacing the outer shell

Many of us have been taught to be very intellectual and very active, and to drive ourselves very hard. We may have a strongly developed intuition, but have not put it in charge. In fact, we may ignore it a lot of the time. We basically protect our sensitive, vulnerable feelings by erecting a tough outer shell. As we begin to use our inner strength and power to take care of ourselves, honor our need for relaxation, and protect our tender feelings, the outer shell melts away and leaves us open yet strong.

I am strong and open.

April 8

Allow your feelings to flow

Acceptance of our feelings is directly related to becoming a creative channel. If you don't allow your feelings to flow, your channel will be blocked. If you've stored up a lot of unfelt or unexpressed emotions, you have a lot of hurt, frightened, angry voices inside which make it difficult to hear the more subtle voice of your intuition. Find a safe place, alone or with a therapist or support group, and allow yourself to express the feelings within you through words, sounds, and/or movement.

I allow my feelings to be expressed and released.

April 9

Change can feel uncomfortable

In being true to yourself you will feel more alive, but you may also feel uncomfortable. This is because you are risking change! As you undergo certain changes, you may experience various intense emotions such as fear, grief, or anger. Allow these emotions expression; after all, your inner guidance has to move through years of accumulated unconsciousness, denial, doubt, and fear. So let your feelings come up and wash through you — you are being cleaned out and healed.

*I accept all the feelings that come
with change and growth.*

Feel more joy

Sadness is related to the opening of your heart. If you allow yourself to feel sad, especially if you can cry, you will find that your heart opens wider and you can feel more love and more joy.

As I allow myself to feel my sadness, I open to more joy.

April 11

Listen to all your feelings

If there seems to be an unhappy or upset feeling inside of you, give it a voice and listen to that emotion. Ask it to talk to you and tell you what it's feeling. Try to hear it and listen to its point of view. Be sympathetic, loving, and supportive towards your feelings. Ask if there is anything you could do to take better care of yourself.

*I love and support
all my feelings today.*

April 12

Experiencing ecstasy

Some of our spiritual models reflect our "good ideas" more than they reveal an actual picture of a conscious life. Many of us want to be mellow, positive, and loving all the time, which really is an expression of our need to feel in control, instead of allowing and trusting our true feelings to show. As we release our need to control, and trust ourselves more and more to allow the full range of our feelings to emerge, we naturally experience the ecstasy of life.

It's safe for me to release control and experience the ecstasy of life.

April 13

Be good to yourself

If I'm feeling sad, I might crawl into bed and cry, taking time to be very loving and nurturing to myself. Or I might find someone caring to talk to who will simply listen to me until some of the feelings are released and I feel lighter. If I've been working too hard, I learn to put work aside no matter how important it seems. I take time to play, or take a hot bath, or read a novel. If someone I love wants something from me that I don't want to give, I learn to say "no," firmly, yet with love. I trust that he or she will be better off than if I did it when I didn't want to. This way when I say "yes" I really mean it.

*I take good care
of myself.*

Renewing our bodies

When we aren't following the flow of energy, life becomes a struggle. Stress and strain take their toll on the physical form. Lines of worry form and the body begins to bend with the effort it is making. If we continue to close off the energy — moment after moment, day after day, year after year — the body may deteriorate more quickly. When we change our pattern and begin to trust ourselves more, the body begins to renew itself and becomes healthier and more energetic.

As I follow the flow of life,
my body grows healthy and vital.

April 15

From mind to body

Creative visualization is a way in which we communicate from our minds to our bodies. It is the process of forming images and thoughts of our desires consciously or unconsciously and then sending them to our bodies as clear messages. Our bodies respond by manifesting those thoughts and images into physical form. The more loving and positive the messages we send, the healthier, stronger, and more vital our bodies become.

I am sending clear, loving thought messages from my mind to my body.

April 16

Love your body

Show your body how much you appreciate and respect it. Your body may have been criticized, judged, and rejected by you for years. It will respond quickly to love and energy. You will feel lighter and more energized. You will start looking more beautiful. Lines in your face will relax. You will glow with strength and health. You will be amazed at the results of loving your body.

*I appreciate, love,
and respect my body.*

April 17

Express the beauty of your spirit

As you find new ways to appreciate your body, you will see it change and become lighter, stronger, more clearly defined, and more beautiful. You will have a sense of the light shining through you. Because your life is your creation and the mirror of your transformation, all forms in your life will increasingly express the power and beauty of your spirit.

My body is a beautiful expression
of my spirit.

April 18

Accept the best

Many of us have difficulty accepting the best. This usually stems from some basic feelings of unworthiness which we took on at a very early age. If you find that you have difficulty imagining yourself in the most wonderful possible circumstances, it might be time to take a good look at your self-image. By accepting and loving yourself, you will be willing and able to accept the best that life has to offer you.

I deserve the very best in my life.

April 19

Self-image

To get in touch with your self-image, begin to ask yourself, "How do I feel about myself right now?" at various times throughout the day. Just begin to notice what kinds of ideas or images you hold in your mind about yourself at different times. Observe whether you frequently tell yourself negative or critical things. Once you understand the ways in which you are not loving yourself, begin to regularly tell yourself positive, appreciative, loving things. Think of specific qualities that you do appreciate about yourself.

I love and appreciate myself as I am now.

April 20

Self-esteem list

Imagine you are your own best friend. Describe yourself exactly as your friend would if he or she was telling someone else about you. Use your own name and tell about all of your good qualities and characteristics. "I can always depend on John when I need help," or "John has a delightful sense of humor and always helps me to laugh when I am taking myself too seriously."

As you do this exercise, either have someone else take notes or write down what you are describing about yourself. Now you have the beginning of your self-esteem list and can add to it daily. The more we love ourselves, the closer we are to our higher self.

*I am becoming
my own best friend.*

April 21

Form — an unfolding creation

Spirit is the energy of the universe, the higher self. Form is the physical world. When our spirit decides to manifest as physical form, we choose a life situation and create a body in accordance with what will best serve and teach us in this lifetime. Ultimately, our goal is to create a form that can do everything our spirit wants to do easily and beautifully. However, it takes time to manifest form. So we must have patience and love for the unfolding creative process.

*I respect and love my form
as my creation.*

April 22

Remembering who we are

After we are born, we forget who we really are and why we came here. We take on the "survival consciousness" of the physical world and we get lost in the world of form. We lose touch with our true power and our spiritual origin. Life becomes a tremendous struggle to find meaning and satisfaction. More and more we are remembering our connection to the divine and beginning to feel the presence of the higher power in our lives.

I am a beautiful spirit, creating a beautiful form.

April 23

We have everything we need

We can learn to live in the world of form — our physical bodies, personalities, and physical surroundings — without losing touch with our connection to spirit. We can have everything the world has to offer, yet be willing to let go of it when we need to. Because the universe within us is rich and powerful, we come to know intuitively that we have everything we need.

I can let go and trust because I know I have everything I need within.

April 24

Recognize both spirit and form

The first step in the process of consciously integrating form and spirit is to be able to recognize and feel both the consciousness of your spirit and the consciousness of your form. Spirit may want to race ahead, so it has to learn to go at the pace the form can handle.

I can feel both my form and my spirit.

Integrate your form and spirit

love and accept both aspects of yourself — form *and* spirit. They are both beautiful and vital parts of you. Without your spirit you wouldn't be alive, and without your form you wouldn't be able to exist in the physical world. You'd be existing in some other realm of consciousness. The basic key to integrating spirit and form is learning to listen to your intuition and acting on it.

I love and accept both my body and spirit.

April 26

Create a balance within

S it comfortably with your back straight. Close your eyes. Relax your body completely. Imagine there is a long cord from the base of your spine extending down through the floor into the earth. This is called a grounding cord. Now imagine that the energy of the earth is flowing up through this cord, through all parts of your body, and out through the top of your head. Now imagine that the energy of the cosmos is flowing in through the top of your head, through your body, down through the grounding cord and your feet, and into the earth. Feel both these flows going in different directions and mixing harmoniously in your body. This creates a balance which will increase your sense of well-being, your power of manifestation.

I am grounded and centered.

April 27

Learning to channel your higher self

Almost any form of meditation will eventually take you to an experience of yourself as source, or your "higher self." If you are not sure what this experience is, just continue to practice relaxation, visualization, and affirmation. Eventually you will start to experience certain moments during your meditation when there is a shift in your consciousness and you feel as though things are really working. You may feel energy flowing through you, or a warm, radiant glow in your body. You are beginning to channel the energy of your higher self.

I am more and more in touch with my higher self.

Be patient with yourself

When you first become aware of the experience of your higher self, you may be feeling strong, clear, and creative at one moment, and then be thrown back into confusion and insecurity at the next moment. This seems to be a natural part of the process. At these times it is really important to love yourself while you are feeling these extremes.

I trust
my own process.

April 29

You have a friend

 $\mathcal{E}$ ach one of us has all the wisdom and knowledge we will ever need right within us. It is available to us through our intuitive mind. One of the best ways to connect with this inner wisdom is by meeting and getting to know our guide, counselor, imaginary friend, or inner being. You can think of it as a person or being whom you can talk to and relate to as a wise and loving friend.

I have a wise and loving friend within me.

April 30

Meeting your inner guide

Close your eyes and relax deeply. Go to your inner sanctuary. Imagine that you are standing on a path. Start to walk up the path. See in the distance a form coming toward you radiating a clear bright light. As you approach the form, see how it looks, how it is dressed, whether it is male or female. Greet this being, ask its name. Take whatever name comes. Ask if there is anything he or she would like to say to you. You may ask specific questions. When the experience of being together feels complete, thank your guide. Express your appreciation and ask him or her to meet you again, whenever you desire.

I am now in contact with a wise inner guide.

May 1

Put your inner female in the guiding position

$\mathcal{E}$ach of us, man or woman, has within us an inner male *and* an inner female. The inner female acts as your intuition, the door to your higher intelligence. Your male listens to her and acts to support her feelings. The true function of male energy is to provide absolute clarity, directness, and a passionate strength based on what your intuitive feelings, coming through your female, tell you.

In order to live a harmonious and creative life, you need to have both your inner female and male energies fully developed and functioning correctly together. To fully integrate the inner male and female, you need to put your inner female, your intuition, in the guiding position, with the male supporting her.

My inner male is now acting to support my inner female.

May 2

Shifting from fear to trust

The feminine power, the power of the spirit, is always within us. It is up to the male energy to determine how we relate to that power. We can fight it, block it, attempt to control it, try to keep ourselves separate from it, or we can trust and open up to it, learn to support it and move with it. Individually and collectively, we are shifting from a position of fear and control to a position of surrender and trust of the intuitive.

My inner male totally supports, loves, and expresses my female intuition.

May 3

Wholeness within

We may not realize that the basic functions of feminine and masculine energies exist in each person. We usually tend to associate male and female energies with their respective body types. From this perspective each person would be only half a person, dependent on the other half for its very existence. As we cannot live effectively in the world without the full range of masculine and feminine energies, each sex has felt helplessly dependent on the other for its very survival. Now, as we are becoming aware of both male and female qualities within us, a deep sense of wholeness can emerge for each individual.

I accept both the masculine and feminine energies within me; I feel whole.

May 4

Expressing power directly

Our female power cannot move directly into the physical world without the support of our male action. Without it, our power is suppressed and must come out indirectly through manipulative patterns or physical symptoms or in sudden unfocused ways — emotional outbursts, even acts of violence. As we practice stating our feelings and needs directly, the need to manipulate falls away and we begin to feel our inherent power.

*I now acknowledge
and express my power directly.*

May 5

Changing old views

We are changing our way of looking at the world. In our culture, we have used our male energy, our ability to think and act, to suppress and control our feminine intuition, rather than to support and express her. I call this traditional patriarchal use of the male energy the "old" male, and it exists equally in men and women. Now we can begin to use our male energy in a different way by supporting and listening to our feminine intuition.

I now use my male energy to express my intuitive guidance.

May 6

Nurturing from within

Traditionally, men have been disconnected from their female energy, thereby disconnected from life, power, and love.

Men have been out there in the world secretly feeling helpless, alone, and empty, although they must pretend to be in control and powerful. They seek nurturing and inner connection through women, but when they connect with their own female, they receive her incredible love from within themselves.

My inner female is nurturing me with incredible love.

May 7

Support from within

Traditionally, women have been in touch with their female energy — intuition and feeling — but they haven't backed her up with their male energy. They have not acknowledged what they know inside. They have acted as if they were powerless, yet they are really very powerful. They have sought external support and validation from men. As women claim their inner male and allow him to support their female energy, they feel both feminine and powerful.

My inner male supports and validates me.

May 8

We value ourselves

All of us, men and women alike, have gone after external validation rather than valuing what we know and who we are. As we learn to balance the female intuition with male action, we move from a state of helplessness to a state of power. We then are no longer so dependent on validation from others because we are giving it to ourselves.

I value who I am.

May 9

Validating yourself

ere is an exercise to help you begin appreciating and validating yourself:

Stand in front of the mirror and look directly in your eyes. In a clear strong voice make this statement to yourself, "*(Your first name)*, one thing I really like about you is..." and complete the sentence with something that you appreciate about yourself. It could be a quality of your personality, an aspect of your appearance, or something you've done that you feel proud of. Repeat this process at least ten times, mentioning a different positive attribute each time.

If possible, do this exercise every day for at least a week, and once a week after that.

I like myself.

May 10

Your relationship with yourself

𝓘n "old world" relationships, the focus was on the other person and on the relationship itself. You communicated for the purpose of trying to get the other person to understand you, to give you more of what you needed. In "new world" relationships, the main focus is on building your relationship with yourself and the universe. You communicate your feelings primarily in order to keep your channel clear, so the life force can keep flowing freely through you.

I am now building a loving relationship with myself and the universe.

May 11

No need to sacrifice

Most people believe that sacrifice and compromise arc necessary to preserve a relationship. This is based on a misunderstanding of the nature of the universe. The universe is loving and abundant, and we can all receive everything we truly need without sacrificing what is important to us. As we learn to feel and express our needs honestly and clearly to ourselves and to our loved ones, we naturally begin to listen more deeply to the needs of others. On the surface there often seems to be conflict between our needs and those of others, but with patience and honesty we will discover an underlying truth in which each person can have his/her needs fulfilled.

I express my needs honestly,
listen to the needs of others,
and look for the deepest truth.

May 12

Loving all parts of ourselves

It is important to accept and experience all of our feelings, including the so-called negative ones, without attempting to change them. At the same time we can create a new point of view about ourselves by embracing and loving all parts of ourselves, not just the parts we already like. As we embrace and express our feelings, we create an intimate and loving relationship with ourselves.

*I accept and experience
all my feelings.*

May 13

Express yourself directly

If you are always "waiting" to be, do, or have what you want, your energy becomes blocked. Your body may reflect this in excess "weight" or other physical problems. Express yourself directly. Set clear boundaries with other people and do what you need to do to take good care of yourself. Energy will then move freely through your body and this circulation will help to dissolve excess weight. The more you are willing to be yourself, the less you'll need to use food as a substitute nurturer. You will be receiving the natural nurturing of the universe.

It is healthy to express myself clearly and directly.

May 14

Reclaiming our power

When we suppress our natural power to express ourselves and make choices, allowing people to have undue power over us, we feel helpless and victimized. This makes us angry. Because we are frightened of our anger, we tend to suppress it, deadening our other emotions as well. For many people who are becoming more conscious, getting in touch with anger is a very positive sign. It means we are reclaiming our power.

As I feel my anger,
I reclaim my power.

May 15

Mastery of our lives

When feeling angry, take whatever practical steps are necessary in order to take care of yourself, express your needs, or set your boundaries. But don't focus excessively on the external problems. Instead allow yourself to recognize that it is the loss of your power you feel angry about. As we get more in touch with our power and express it directly and assertively, we no longer feel helpless and angry. Rather, we accept mastery over our own lives.

I am the master of my life.

May 16

Expressing anger safely

People are often very frightened of their anger. They feel it will cause them to do something harmful. If you have this fear, create a safe situation where you can express your anger, alone or with a trusted therapist or friend. Allow yourself to talk angrily, shout, hit pillows, whatever you feel like. Once you've done this in a safe environment, you will have released some of the charge, and you can look underneath the anger to find what you need to do to take better care of yourself. Like any emotion, anger is a valuable tool, teaching us who we are and how we feel.

I am now creating safe ways and places to express my anger.

May 17

Learn to assert yourself

You transform your anger into personal power by learning to assert yourself. Learn to ask for what you want and do what you want to do without being unduly influenced by other people. When you stop giving your power away to other people, you won't feel the same kind of anger anymore. Instead you will feel clear, strong, and honest.

Today I say what I want to say and do what I want to do.

May 18

Look for the hurt child

If you are a person who has felt and expressed a lot of anger in your life, you can now look for the hurt that is underneath it and express those feelings. You no longer need to use anger as a defense mechanism to avoid being vulnerable. In order to heal your anger, get in touch with the hurt child within you. Learn to love, nurture, and protect that little child.

I'm learning to protect and care for the vulnerable child in me.

May 19

Express hurt feelings directly

*H*urt is an expression of vulnerability. We tend to mask it with defensiveness and blame. It is important to express feelings of hurt directly and if possible, in a non-blaming way. "I felt really hurt when you didn't ask me to go with you," as opposed to "You don't care about my feelings."

Risking the exposure of our true feelings, even hurt or sad feelings, can be scary, but it creates the openness, sharing, and intimacy we crave.

I am embracing and expressing my vulnerability.

May 20

Allow yourself to grieve

*g*rief is an intense form of sadness related to the death or ending of something. It is very important to allow ourselves to grieve fully and not to cut this process short. It can sometimes last a long time, or recur periodically for a very long time. Accept it and give yourself as much support as you need whenever grief comes up. It is a paradox that we cannot truly release or end anything unless we grieve for it. The tears move through us, wash us clean, and create the space for something new.

As I allow myself to grieve, I heal sadness and create space for the new.

May 21

A new level of surrender

Sometimes sadness and grief lead to hopelessness. Hopelessness can lead to surrender. When you feel hopeless, you are giving up and recognizing that none of your old patterns are working. As you allow yourself to really give up and feel the helplessness completely, it will be followed by a new level of surrender to the universe, which brings peace and new hope.

I am surrendering to the universe.

May 22

Small things first

If you are just beginning to learn how to trust and follow your intuition, you probably don't want to leap off a building and hope that you can fly. It is important that you take small steps first. Practice following your intuition in everyday things, trusting your gut feelings moment by moment and acting on them as best you can. As you learn to trust yourself in small matters, you will build power and confidence to take bigger risks and deal with the larger issues in your life successfully.

Step-by-step I am building trust in myself and in the universe.

May 23

Money is a reflection

Money is a symbol representing energy. Your money is a reflection of the energy moving through your channel. The better you learn to operate in the world based on trust in your intuition, the stronger your channel will be and the more likely you are to have enough money for the things you truly need and desire. The money in your life is based on your ability to listen to your inner guidance and risk acting on it. It flows in an easy, effortless, and joyful way because there is no sacrifice involved. You're no longer attached to it. Instead, you can experience the joy of learning how to follow the energy of the universe. Money is just an extra bonus in the process.

As I trust myself,
money comes to me easily.

May 24

Balance your checkbook

When it comes to money, balance is as important as in every other area of our lives. If you have been very careless and casual about money, or have denied the existence or importance of money, you may need to pay more attention to the details of handling it. Learn to balance your checkbook monthly and follow a budget. If you see these practices as helping you to develop your ability to manage money successfully, you will find them interesting. They won't hinder your enjoyment, but will open the way for more energy and money to flow through your life.

I enjoy managing money carefully and successfully.

May 25

Loosen up!

If you've always saved your money and been very careful about spending it, you may need to learn to handle money a little more freely. There's no need to take big risks. Just start with small steps, spending a little more money than you usually would based on any intuitive feelings you might have to give to yourself and others. This will help to create more prosperity and enjoyment in your life.

It's okay for me
to enjoy my money.

May 26

Taking risks with work and money

Be willing to take some modest risks in the areas of work and money. If we do only what we think we *should* do in order to make money and be secure, we won't listen to the intuitive voice that tells us to try something new, to be more creative, or to move on to the next step on our path. When we listen to our intuition and take some risks, we are not alone. The universe will support us and reward us for taking risks on its behalf!

The universe rewards me for trying new things.

May 27

Ideal scene

list any fantasies you've had about work, career, or a creative activity. Write an ideal scene, a description of your perfect job or career as you would like it to be. Write in the present tense with description and detail that make it seem very real. Now, close your eyes and experience how it feels to have your fantasy or ideal scene come true. See yourself having all that you want and notice how your body reacts to this possibility. Remember these feelings as you go through your day, and the steps necessary to make it happen will emerge one by one.

My dreams are coming true.

May 28

Have whatever you truly desire

The universe is naturally abundant. The things you truly need or want are here for the asking. Believe that you can have what you want, truly desire it, and be willing to receive it.

I believe in abundance, I desire abundance, I receive abundance.

The law of attraction

*E*nergy of a certain quality or vibration tends to attract energy of a similar quality and vibration. Thoughts and feelings have their own magnetic energy, which attracts energy of a similar nature. We can see this principle at work, for instance, when we accidentally run into someone we've just been thinking of, or happen to pick up a book which contains the perfect information we need at that moment.

*I am now attracting
everything I need.*

May 30

Expect the best

When we are negative and fearful, insecure or anxious, we tend to attract the very experiences, situations, or people that we are seeking to avoid. We attract these experiences in order to become conscious of and heal our deepest fears. When we are feeling positive in attitude, expecting and envisioning pleasure, satisfaction, and happiness, we tend to attract and create people, situations, and events which conform to these expectations. Therefore, the more we are able to imagine and accept our highest good, the more it begins to manifest in our lives, and the more power and freedom we will feel.

Today I expect pleasure and satisfaction.

May 31

Set monthly goals

Once a month list five or six important goals in your life, things that you would like to be putting your energy into right now, or in the near future. Some of them may be short-term, some may be long-term, but they are the ones you feel most strongly about at the moment. With short-range goals, be realistic; with long-range goals, be expansive and idealistic. They may change from month to month. The purpose of writing your goals is to open up and expand your imagination as well as to help you focus on what things are truly important to you.

*I am expanding
my imagination.*

June 1

Remember to check inside

For me, it is a constant discipline to remember to go back inside to connect with my intuition. I remind myself regularly during the day to do this. If I find myself getting lost in my outer activities, I check inside to see if I am being true to my feelings. This keeps the flow of the universe moving through me.

*I remember to check
with my intuition.*

June 2

More and more of the life force

As we learn to pay attention to our intuitive feelings, follow our own energy and live our truth, we find that we feel more and more of the life force moving through us. That feeling of greater aliveness is so wonderful that it becomes our major focus and source of fulfillment.

I feel the life force moving through me.

June 3

Letting go of attachment to externals

When we're following our own energy, we feel less attached to the externals of our lives. Whether or not things go as we have planned seems less important when we feel that our satisfaction is coming from sustaining our connection to our own life energy. Ironically, when we stay true to ourselves in this way, the externals of our lives reflect our inner integrity. We attract to us and create around us exactly what our hearts and souls truly desire.

As I let go of control,
I draw to me my heart's desires.

Living your truth

From a deep, quiet place, begin to sense the life force within you. Imagine that you are following your own energy, feeling it, trusting it, moving with it in every moment of your life. You are being completely true to yourself, speaking and living your truth. You feel alive and empowered. Imagine that you are expressing your creativity fully and freely, and let yourself enjoy that experience. By being who you are and expressing yourself, you are having a healing and empowering effect on everyone you encounter and on the world around you.

When I'm true to myself, I have a positive effect on the world around me.

June 5

New directions

You can expect that your intuition will lead you in directions that are new and different for you. If you are comfortable in one type of personality or pattern, you will probably be asked to start expressing the opposite. It's good to know this, especially when you're in the process of learning to hear your inner guidance. A good rule might be to "expect the unexpected."

I'm open to discovering new parts of myself.

June 6

Do less

If you are primarily an active doer, your intuition will almost surely lead you in the direction of doing less. Your feelings will tell you to stop, to relax and take a day off (or a week, or six months!), to spend more time alone with yourself, to spend time in nature, to spend time with no plan and no list, and just practice following the energy as you feel it.

I'm learning to relax
and enjoy myself.

June 7

Do more

If you are more comfortable with "being" than doing, you will undoubtedly be pushed by your inner guidance into more action, more expression, more risk-taking in the world. The key for you is to follow your impulses and to try doing things you wouldn't normally do. You don't have to know why you're doing something or see any particular result from it at first. It's important to simply practice acting spontaneously on your feelings, especially when it comes to dealing with people, expressing your creative energy in the world, making money, or anything else you might normally avoid.

*I'm taking action
to express myself in new ways.*

June 8

You are always taken care of

Know that your money is not really yours, but belongs to the universe. You act as a caretaker, or steward for money, using it only as directed to use it by your own intuition. There is no fear of loss when you know that you are always taken care of.

I care for the universe's money and the universe cares for me.

June 9

Giving and receiving

The universe is made up of pure energy, the nature of which is to move and flow. When we tune into the rhythm of the universe, we are able to give and receive freely, knowing that we really never lose anything, but constantly gain. When we give our energy, we make space for more to flow into us. As we give, we also receive.

*I now give
and receive freely.*

June 10

Stay open to that flow

Sometimes when we find ourselves fearful, insecure, worried, or believing in scarcity, we cut off the wonderful flow of energy from the universe. The abundant energy of the universe flows to us in many forms: love, affection, appreciation, money, material possessions, and friendship, to name a few.

It is important to keep our consciousness open to receiving all the blessings the universe has for us.

I am open to receive universal energy in all its forms.

June 11

Giving is fun

The more we have given to ourselves, the more we have to give to others. When we find that place within ourselves that is giving, we begin to create an outward flow. Giving to others comes not from a sense of sacrifice, self-righteousness, or some concept we have of spirituality, but for the pure pleasure of it, because it's fun. True giving can only come from a full, loving space.

As I give to myself, it is fun to give to others.

June 12

The outflow-inflow principle

As we outflow our loving energy, we make room for more and more to flow into us. And the more you share of yourself, the more you seem to get from the world, because of the outflow-inflow principle. As you outflow, you create a space into which something must inflow. Giving becomes its own reward. Remember always that you can't continue to give unless you are equally open to receiving. Giving also includes giving to yourself.

As I give, I receive.

Give love and appreciation

Sit down right now and make a list of people to whom you would like to give love and appreciation, and think of a way that you can do so to each one within the next week. This could be by touching, making a phone call, sending a gift, giving money, anything that makes you feel good. Practice speaking more words of thanks, appreciation, and admiration to people.

I give love and appreciation to others.

June 14

Find what's right for you

The way to a beautiful, strong healthy body is to learn to trust and love yourself. You can begin the process by becoming aware of all the "rules" you have heard about how you should look, what you should eat, how you should exercise, and so on.

Once you gain awareness of these rules, you can begin to tune into your own intuitive feelings about what is *really* right for you.

I am discovering what's right for me.

June 15

Your body knows

Your own body and your intuition are, ultimately the best guides about what is good for you and how to take care of yourself. Your body will let you know what it needs to eat and how it wants to move and exercise. If you need more information or structure, your inner guidance may help you find the appropriate class, book, nutritionist, exercise coach, or whatever is needed.

My body knows
what it needs.

June 16

Trust yourself

People generally react with fear when I suggest that they trust themselves and follow their body's needs. They are afraid they will stay in bed all day, eat chocolates, and get fat. If you have food addictions, be sure to get counseling and group support to discover the underlying causes and to stop the addictive behavior. Practice listening to and following what your body *really* wants. Trust yourself. You will start to look and feel as your spirit is — alive and energized, beautiful and young.

*I trust my body,
I trust myself.*

June 17

Facing our unconsciousness

As we risk expressing ourselves more freely and honestly, some of what comes out will be unpolished, distorted, foolish, or thoughtless. As we learn to act on our inner feelings, all the ways we've blocked ourselves in the past come to awareness and are cleared out. In this process, we have to be willing to face our lack of awareness without self-judgment, but with compassion for ourselves. In this way we can clear our distortions and become more conscious beings.

I accept and express the way I feel.

June 18

We need the reflections

Taking care of yourself does not mean "doing it all alone." Creating a good relationship with yourself is not done in a vacuum, without relationship to other people. If it were, we could all become hermits for a few years until we had a perfect relationship with ourselves, and then just emerge and suddenly have perfect relationships with others. We need to build and strengthen our relationship with ourselves in the world of form through interaction with other people.

My relationships with others help me build my relationship with myself.

The stronger the attraction,
the stronger the mirror

I have found that when I am willing to trust and follow my energy it leads me into relationships with people from whom I have the most to learn. The stronger the attraction, the stronger the mirror. My energy will often lead me to the most intense learning situation. I don't need to enter or stay in a relationship that is not good for me, but if I choose to leave I can still acknowledge the gift and the teaching I received.

I accept my relationships
as my teachers.

June 20

Acknowledging our need

It is the hidden, unacknowledged needs that cause us to seem needy. They don't come out directly, but are expressed indirectly, or telepathically. Other people feel them and back away from us because they intuitively know they can't help us if we aren't acknowledging our need for help. It's paradoxical that we actually become stronger as we recognize and acknowledge our own needs and ask for help directly. People find it easier to give to us, and we feel more and more whole.

I am recognizing and expressing my needs.

Finding our own fulfillment

Other people are seldom able to fulfill our needs consistently, so we become disappointed and frustrated. We either try to change others, which never works, or resign ourselves to accept less than we really want. When another person disappoints us, it may be a message that it's time to look to ourselves for fulfillment and satisfaction at that moment. We may need to express our honest feelings to the other person clearly and simply, and then let go and look within for guidance about what we need to do for ourselves.

I'm learning to take care of myself.

June 22

You are unique

I foresee a time when each person can truly be a unique entity with his or her own free-flowing style of expression. Each relationship will be a unique connection between two beings, taking its individual form and expression. No stereotypes will be possible because each one of us is so individual when we follow the flow of our own energy.

I am unique and
each of my relationships is unique.

June 23

Children are powerful, spiritual beings

I have met a lot of parents who, now that they have become more aware, feel much guilt and sadness in looking back at how they've raised their children. Remember that children are powerful, spiritual beings who are responsible for their own lives. They chose you as a parent so they could learn the things they needed to learn in this lifetime.

I take responsibility for my life choices and I allow others to take responsibility for theirs.

June 24

Children copy what we do

Children do not need us to behave perfectly. They do need us to create an example of how to live effectively in the world of form. They need our imperfect "humanness." As we live our lives, they watch us and notice how we express our feelings and our dreams, and they imitate us. Being very perceptive and pragmatic, they copy what we actually do, not what we say. The more we are true to ourselves, the more we give them permission to be true to themselves.

As I learn to be myself,
I inspire others to be themselves.

June 25

Support their power

Many people hold an underlying attitude that children are helpless or untrustworthy and that parents are completely responsible for controlling and molding them. Children, of course, pick up this attitude and reflect it in their behavior — acting more helpless than they really are, or behaving in an untrustworthy manner. If you recognize children as powerful, spiritually mature beings, they will act accordingly, as will your friends and your family. Affirm these positive attributes daily for yourself and everyone around you.

I recognize my loved ones as powerful, capable, responsible beings.

June 26

Allow yourself safety and support

We have to learn to use our powerful male energy to listen to, trust, and support our female energy. This allows us the safety and support to risk opening and expressing the full range of our feelings. We can be sensitive, receptive, and vulnerable, and are at the same time, stronger, more alive, and more powerful than ever before.

The more I support and trust my feelings, the stronger and more open I am.

June 27

Let your power shine

In the traditional female role, a woman may learn to use her male energy to deny and suppress her natural female power. This leaves her helpless, dependent on men, emotionally unbalanced, and able to express her power only indirectly through manipulation. She may be afraid that if men found out how powerful she really is, they would abandon her. So she carefully keeps her power hidden. As we come to trust and take care of ourselves, it feels safer to risk being a powerful, creative person.

It is safe for me
to be powerful.

June 28

Express positive male power

Many very conscious men have chosen to connect deeply with their feminine energy and yet, in doing so, have disconnected from their male. They have rejected the old macho image and have no other concept of male energy to relate to. These men are usually afraid of their male energy. They feel it will burst forth with the mindlessness and violence they equate with maleness. Thus they lose the positive, assertive male qualities as well. As men begin to find the balance of the female and male energies within, they will realize that their strength and assertiveness is being safely and accurately guided by their intuition.

It is safe for me to express my male energy.

We are becoming more responsible

We are now learning to rely on and validate ourselves instead of abandoning the responsibility and depending on someone else to do it for us. Because the dependency on validation from others is a deep-seated pattern that has endured for centuries, it takes time to change it. The key is for us to just keep listening to, trusting in, and acting on our deepest feelings, while loving and approving of ourselves as much as we can.

I accept the responsibility of listening to and loving myself.

June 30

Create a treasure map

A treasure map is an actual physical picture of a desired goal. It works along the same lines as a blueprint for a building. You can draw it, paint it, or make a collage with magazine pictures and photos. Simple, childlike treasure maps are very effective and fun to do. Basically, it should show you in your ideal scene with your goal fully realized. Include all the elements without getting too complicated. Use lots of color. Include some symbol of the infinite which has meaning and power for you. Put affirmations on your treasure map. This creative process is a powerful physical step toward manifesting your goal.

This or something better is now manifesting for me in totally satisfying and harmonious ways.

Summer

July 1

Attachment to goals

*I*f you have a great deal of attachment to a particular goal, it may interfere with your ability to manifest it. Often, when there is a strong attachment to something, there is a great deal of fear underneath — fear of not getting what we need.

It's perfectly okay to creatively visualize something to which you have a lot of attachment. If it doesn't work out, realize that your own inner conflict may be sending out conflicting messages. Relax and accept your feelings. Understand that resolving the inner conflict is probably an important part of growth for you and a wonderful opportunity to look more closely at your own attitude about life.

*I relax and accept
my feelings.*

July 2

Blocked energy can be released

Creative power has to filter through our beliefs, attitudes, emotions, and habits. The more negative and constricted our beliefs and patterns are, the more they block the creative energy. Most people hope that by ignoring negativity, it will go away, but the reverse is actually true. Through recognizing, acknowledging, and experiencing it, the blocked energy can be released. You are then free to replace it with positive beliefs and attitudes.

Through recognizing and acknowledging my blocks, I release and clear them.

July 3

A clearing process

ere is a basic clearing process that you can use to clear out negative beliefs in order to attain a goal. First, state your goal in the form of an affirmation. Second, write "The reasons I can't have what I want are:" and then start listing every thought that comes into your head. Third, decide which of the negative statements have the most power over you, and make a mark by those. Write an affirmation to counteract each one. Meditate on these affirmations every day along with your original goal.

I am now clearing my negative beliefs.

Declare your independence

The key to independence lies in knowing that at every moment, in every instance, we are creating our life. The more we acknowledge this truth, the more power and freedom we experience.

Rather than blaming ourselves or others for the things we do not like in our life, we now realize we are manifesting our reality and have the power to change it.

Our life is a reflection of what we believe we deserve. As we deepen our acceptance of and open ourselves to the infinite love of the universe, a new power flows through us, releasing us from the bondage of our old way of life.

I feel the freedom and power to create the life I desire.

July 5

Let go and ask

In certain situations you may try to do affirmations and find that you simply can't do them, or if you do, it feels like you aren't accomplishing anything. In that case, it may be time for you to let go of what you were trying to do. Get in touch with your inner guidance and ask what to do next. You have access to an ever present resource within that will guide you to your next step.

I am asking my inner guidance to show me my next step.

July 6

Learning to follow the spirit within

$\mathcal{I}$am learning to follow the spirit within me, wherever it wants to take me. Every time I check in, feeling the energy inside me and letting it direct me, I find this a wonderful way to live. When I do this, I experience joy, power, love, peace, and excitement.

I am learning to follow the spirit within me.

July 7

Increasing our aliveness

$\mathcal{E}$very time we don't trust ourselves and our inner truth, we decrease our aliveness. Our bodies will reflect this with numbness, pain, and a loss of vitality.

Every time we allow the energy of the universe to move through us by trusting and following our intuition, we increase our sense of aliveness. Our bodies will reflect this with health, beauty, and vitality.

I trust my inner truth
and I feel vibrantly alive.

July 8

Unblock the flow

When we are blocking the flow of energy, we begin to experience less and less vitality. As the flow diminishes, our bodies are slow to revitalize. They begin to age and deteriorate. Poor posture, tight jaws, headaches, and backaches are all reflections of chronic energy blocks.

By relaxing and nurturing ourselves, by healing our emotional wounds, by reaching for what gives us joy, we can release these patterns from our lives. In turn, our bodies will experience a new ease and new power.

I relax and nurture myself.

Notice how you feel

$\mathcal{G}$et in a comfortable position. Close your eyes. Breathe deeply. Relax your body and your mind. Recall a recent situation in which you did not do what you wanted to do. Replay this scene in your mind. Notice how you looked and felt physically, emotionally, and spiritually. Now go back and see yourself doing exactly what you'd like in that situation. Notice how your body feels. Notice how you look, and how you feel about yourself. Spend a few minutes feeling what it's like to trust yourself and act on your desires.

I trust myself and I act on that trust.

July 10

Keep a journal

Keep a journal of some of the decisions you make during the day. Notice when you do what you want, when you choose not to, and for what reasons. For example, you may choose to go to a party when you really want to stay home. Do you push yourself to work hard even if you are not feeling well? Do you hold back from expressing your ideas, feelings, or creative impulses out of fear of criticism?

Write how you feel about the choices you made. Notice how you felt physically and emotionally. Be careful not to judge or criticize yourself for any of your choices. Cultivate an attitude of compassionate observation so you can learn what works for you and what doesn't.

Today I pay attention to how I feel about the choices I make.

July 11

Achieving balance

The feminine (spiritual) energy is a powerful force that moves us toward union and oneness. The masculine energy (personality) defines our individuality. Both are equally necessary and important for living successfully in the physical world.

As we learn to trust, honor, and express our feminine and masculine energies in harmony with each other, we feel our oneness with all of life and at the same time we appreciate and respect our uniqueness. This helps us to achieve balance in every aspect of our lives.

I am a unique individual and I am one with the universe.

July 12

Communion

I often find the most powerful communion with the universe when I am alone, especially out in nature. At such times, the places inside of me that sometimes feel empty are filled with the energy of spirit. Here I find a guiding presence that nudges me in the direction I need to go, and helps me to learn the lesson that lies in taking each step along my path.

Nature helps me connect with spirit.

July 13

A powerful presence

Imagine that there is a very powerful presence within you. This presence is totally loving, strong, and wise. It is nurturing, protecting, guiding, and caring for you. At times it can be very strong and forceful. It can also be very light, joyful, and playful. As you get to know and trust it, it will make your life exciting, meaningful, and fulfilling. Relax and enjoy the feeling or thought that you are being totally taken care of by the universe.

I feel and trust the presence of the universe in my life.

July 14

Flow

Most of us have had experiences at certain times when we've felt life energy, wisdom, and power flow through us, when we have felt momentarily "enlightened." We have a brief moment of clarity and power and then it goes away again. When it goes away, we feel lost and unsure of ourselves. This is a natural part of the human experience. The more you practice trusting and following your intuition, the more consistently you will feel that sense of "flow."

I'm in the flow.

July 15

Let things fall apart

As you strengthen the commitment to trusting yourself, everything in your life may change. At first, as you begin to let go of your old patterns, it may appear that things in your life are falling apart. You may find that you have to let go of certain things you've been attached to.

Of course, these changes can be upsetting and frightening. Over time, however, you will find that this is all part of the transformation you are going through. As you learn to be true to yourself, you will find that you attract people, work, and other circumstances that reflect your evolution and development.

*I am letting go
and staying open.*

July 16

Our own special path

.

When instead of following our own intuitive knowingness, we follow the behavior we have observed in others or attempt to follow the rules and regulations laid down by others, we move in ways that are counter to our own natural flow. This means we are not acting on what *we* know. We are not saying and doing what we really feel. As we learn to pay attention, we begin to see the difference between old messages from others and our own natural signals. The more we listen to and trust ourselves, the more our own special path unfolds magically before us.

Today I follow my own path.

July 17

Our body is our primary creation

Our body is the vehicle we have created to express us in the physical world. It's like a semi-formed piece of clay that molds itself to show the patterns of energy moving through it. The body is our primary feedback mechanism which can show us what is and isn't working about our ways of thinking, expressing, and living. As we live our truth more fully and freely, our body grows healthier, stronger, and more beautiful.

My body beautifully expresses
who I am.

July 18

A solid base of trust

We are unafraid to the same degree that we experience the presence of the universe in our own body. Every time we open ourselves up to more power, more of the old fear gets flushed to the surface and released. In the healing process we experience alternating states of power and fear. Gradually, a solid base of trust is established within us. The more light we allow within us, the brighter the world we live in will be.

I am building a solid base of trust within.

July 19

What I am right now

If we pretend to be more enlightened than we really are, we will miss an opportunity to heal ourselves. Admitting our limitations can make us feel vulnerable, yet it is very freeing.

We just have to be ourselves as we are now, accepting the mixture of enlightened awareness and human limitations that is in each of us. Through this self-acceptance, we find a deep peace and self-love.

Today I accept myself
as I am.

July 20

Forgiving and releasing

Write down the names of everyone in your life toward whom you feel or have felt resentment, hurt, or anger. Write down what they did to you and what you resent them for. Then close your eyes, relax, and visualize each person. Explain to them what you have felt angry about, and share with them the hurt beneath the anger. Tell them that now you are going to do your best to dissolve and release all constricted energy between you. Give them a blessing and say, "I forgive you and release you. Go your own way and be happy." If there is someone you are not yet ready to forgive or release, that's okay too. In time you will.

I am forgiving and releasing everyone.

July 21

Forgiving yourself

Write down the names of everyone you think of in your life whom you feel you have hurt and what you did to them. Close your eyes, relax, and imagine each person. Tell him or her what you did and ask them to forgive you and give you their blessing. Then picture them doing so. When you have finished this process, write, "I forgive myself and release my feelings of guilt." Do this as often as you need to.

I forgive myself.

July 22

Listen to your own needs

What does it mean to take care of yourself? It means trusting and following your intuition, taking time to listen to all of your feelings including the feelings of the child within you that is sometimes hurt or scared. It means responding with caring, love, and appropriate action. It means putting your most important inner needs first and trusting that everyone else's needs will get taken care of, that everything that needs to be done will be handled. It means trusting that the universe is looking after each and every one of us.

Today I am listening and responding to my own needs.

July 23

We are spontaneous beings

Any healthy child who has a reasonably positive environment has a body filled with beauty and vitality. The natural life energy of the universe flows freely through, unimpeded by negative habits.

In a supportive environment, we are totally spontaneous beings. We eat when we are hungry, fall asleep when we are tired, and express exactly what we feel, so the energy doesn't get blocked. We are constantly renewed and revitalized by our own natural energy.

I am a natural, spontaneous being.

Young children are our clearest mirrors

Young children are often our clearest mirrors because as intuitive beings, they are tuned in on a feeling level and respond honestly to every situation. They haven't learned to cover up their feelings yet. When we as adults do not speak or behave according to what we are actually feeling, children pick up the discrepancy immediately and react to it. Watching their reactions can help us become more aware of our own suppressed feelings.

I am becoming more aware of my feelings.

Children need honesty

Many parents think they have to protect their children from their (the parents') confusion or so-called negative feelings. They think that being a good parent means always maintaining a certain role: being patient, loving, wise, and strong. But in fact, children need honesty. They need to see a human being experience the full range of human emotion and be honest about it. This gives children permission to support and love themselves as natural and truthful beings.

Today I am giving the gift of my honesty.

July 26

Recognizing old patterns

We begin very early to develop habits that run counter to our natural energy, habits that are designed to help us survive in the neurotic world in which we find ourselves. We pick up these patterns from our families, friends, teachers, and the community in general. Eventually we begin to see that these habits are no longer serving us. Through becoming aware of them, we take the first and most important step toward changing them.

*It is safe for me
to let go of old habits.*

July 27

Change happens through awareness

Old patterns don't change overnight. Sometimes we keep doing the same things and getting the same unpleasant results long after we think we should know better! Change happens not by trying to *make* yourself change, but by becoming conscious of what's *not* working.

Through increased awareness, eventually you will begin to respond differently.

With awareness,
my old patterns are transforming.

July 28

Get the message

If there are problems in your life, it means the universe is trying to get your attention. It's saying, "Hey, there's something you need to be aware of, something that needs to be changed here." If you don't pay attention, the problems will intensify, until you finally get the message and start to listen more carefully to your inner guidance. If you learn to pay attention to small signals, you will learn from them and your problems will gradually be solved.

I listen to the small signals and learn from them.

July 29

Ask your inner guidance

It does not always help to think about or analyze problems with your rational mind. Sometimes it is far more effective to turn to your inner guidance, to ask the higher power of the universe for help. Simply sit quietly. Take a few deep breaths and focus your awareness within. Ask your inner wisdom, either silently or aloud, for guidance or help in solving the problem. You may or may not get an immediate answer. Go about your life, but stay open and pay attention to your gut feelings. As you get a sense of what feels right, act on this feeling.

My inner wisdom gives me guidance and direction.

July 30

Create the space for intimacy

As I learn to love myself, I automatically receive the love and appreciation from others that I desire. My willingness to be intimate with my own deep feelings creates the space for intimacy with another. As I feel the power of the universe flowing through me, I create a life of passion and fulfillment which I can share with others.

I am willing to be intimate with my own deep feelings.

July 31

The quality of love

Close your eyes. Deeply relax. When you feel re-laxed and energized, say, "I now call forth the quality of love." Feel the energy of love coming to you from someplace inside of you, filling you up and radiating out from you. Remain for a few minutes experiencing this feeling. Then if you wish, direct it toward anyone to whom you wish to send a blessing.

*I now call forth
the quality of love.*

August 1

Celebrate your gifts

If you are having trouble deciding just what it is that you are supposed to be doing with your life, pay attention to what energizes you, what excites you and brings you joy. Choose to allow your channel to function as it wishes. Energy will flow through you and skills will come easily as the universe moves to support you in the celebration and expression of your gifts.

I express my gifts easily and skillfully.

August 2

Exploring our fantasies

At times fantasies can tell us how we really want to be expressing ourselves. We sometimes have a strong sense of what we would like to do, yet we take up a very different career. We feel we need a career that is more practical or will gain the approval of our parents or the world.

In the past we have felt it was impossible to do what we really wanted. We are now seeing that when we do what we really want we gain our own approval. We experience our own vitality and freedom. Today we can risk exploring things that really turn us on.

I now risk exploring things that excite me.

August 3

Get in touch with your fantasies

Most people do have some sense of what they would love to be doing, but this feeling is often repressed and is experienced only in the form of some wildly impractical fantasy. There is truth in your desire, even if it seems impossible. It is telling you something about some part of you that is wanting to come forth. See if you can take one small, simple step toward letting that part of you be expressed.

I pay attention to my fantasies and look for the truth within them.

Follow the impulse

*F*ollow any impulse that you have in the direction of your true work/play desires. Even if it seems unrealistic, follow the impulse anyway. For example, if you are sixty-five years old and have always wanted to dance, imagine you are a dancer. At home alone, put on some music and dance freely in whatever way feels good to your body. This will get you in touch with a part of yourself that wants and needs expression. You may end up dancing much more than you thought possible and you may be led to other and different forms of expression that will feel wonderful.

I am now following
my creative impulses.

August 5

Learning can be fun

The learning process can be full of joy, fun, and excitement. We can experience it as a wonderful adventure. We no longer need to sacrifice and struggle in the moment to have what we want in the future. The journey and the destination become one and the same. Learning new skills, going to school, exploring untried talents — any of these can be fun and fulfilling if you are following your intuition.

I'm having fun learning.

August 6

Imagine a fabulous career

*G*et comfortable. Close your eyes. Breathe deeply, relaxing your body and your mind. Imagine you are doing exactly what you want in your life. You have a fabulous career that is fun and fulfilling. You are doing what you've always fantasized about doing and getting well paid for it. You feel relaxed, energized, creative, and powerful. You follow your intuition from moment to moment and are richly rewarded for it. You are doing exactly what you want to be doing.

I am making a good living doing exactly what I want to do.

Lives will be transformed

Whether you are washing the dishes, taking a walk, or building a house, if you are doing it with a sense of being where you want to be and doing what you want to be doing, the fullness of that experience will be felt by those around you. They will sense the completeness of your experience and their lives will be transformed to the degree that they are ready to allow the impact of that experience to affect them.

My joy is felt by everyone around me.

August 8

You can transform others

If you walk into a room loving yourself, knowing that you are a creative channel, and expressing yourself honestly, everyone in the room can be affected, even though they may not be aware of it. As a direct result of your presence, you will see others become more alive and empowered. It is an incredibly exciting and satisfying experience.

*I am one with my self,
a channel for the universe.*

August 9

We are not alone

Once we accept the reality of a higher power operating in the universe, channeled through our intuition, it becomes clear that our personal problems, and even world problems, are actually caused by not respecting that intuition. Personal and social problems are a result of fear and the suppression of our intuition.

We are not alone with our problems. We can rely on our intuition as if it were a great and wise friend accompanying us on this journey through life — watching out for us, helping us, loving us. We can practice following our intuition with the certainty that we are loved and cared for.

I am guided by my higher power at all times.

August 10

Change occurs naturally

If you feel your progress toward your goals is too slow, ask the universe for help. Remind yourself that things will always change in time. Change happens not by forcing it, but by becoming aware of what's not working in your life and being willing to let it go. Change, a dynamic, natural process, is always occurring, even when we're not aware of it.

I allow things to change in their own natural time.

August 11

Giving consciously

At this point, we may realize that it doesn't work to try to take care of ourselves by taking care of others. I'm the only one who can actually take good care of me, so I might as well do it directly and allow others to do the same thing for themselves. This doesn't mean we can't care for and give to others; it means that we make a conscious choice to give or not, based on what we truly feel rather than out of fear or obligation. In fact, the better we take care of ourselves, the more we have to give.

When I take care of myself,
I have more to give.

August 12

Assert yourself consistently

One of the most important keys to creating a healthy, beautiful body is learning to assert yourself consistently in your life. Many people with body issues have a pattern of doubting themselves, of being afraid to trust their feelings and act on them. They especially need to learn how to say "no" to others when they don't want to do something. When our first priority is to please and take care of others, we are denying who we really are and what we really feel. When we are afraid to be true to ourselves, our bodies serve us by reflecting these fears, so we can become conscious of them and heal them.

Today I am willing to assert myself.

Take action

The key to asserting yourself is to take action on your feelings and intuition. I have seen people begin to lose weight or become physically healthier simply by doing something they've been afraid to do, or by expressing some feeling they've suppressed. By becoming more assertive, underweight people become more willing to take up space in the world. By continuing to speak and act your truth, you will dissolve blocks and find your proper weight.

*I now take action
on my feelings.*

August 14

Risk asserting yourself

At first the prospect of asserting yourself moment to moment can be frightening. We are not used to stating what we need and taking the action necessary to give it to ourselves. It takes a conscious effort for us to tune in to how we feel and to risk doing it. But once you start, you'll want to keep doing it. You will have more energy and look more radiant.

It is safe for me to assert my needs and feelings.

August 15

Balancing weight easily and naturally

Once overweight people learn true assertion, they are often able to lose weight easily and naturally, without any type of deprivation. The increased energy circulating in their bodies dissolves the blocked energy and the extra weight gradually melts away. They do not need it for strength or protection so they release it effortlessly.

By the same process of assertion, underweight people release their fear, and are able to take in more life and more nourishment. If any particular food plan is needed, they will be intuitively led to an appropriate nutritional consultant and diet.

As I trust and assert
my feelings, I create a healthy,
beautiful body.

August 16

It is our birthright

We have spent many years believing it is necessary to compromise and sacrifice for others. We have long carried the belief that "you can't have everything." We fear we have no right to our feelings and desires.

It is absolutely our birthright to have the things our hearts and souls truly desire, and to find satisfaction and fulfillment in our lives.

I deserve love, happiness, and prosperity.

August 17

Being a good parent

Our old ideas of parenting usually involved feeling totally responsible for the welfare of our children and following some specific standards of behavior. As you learn to trust yourself and be yourself, you may find that you are violating many of your old rules about what a good parent does. Yet the vibrant energy that is coming through you, your increasing sense of satisfaction in your life, and your trust of yourself and the universe will do far more to help your children than anything else possibly could.

My loved ones benefit when I trust and be myself.

August 18

Those you love will be positively affected

As we learn to fulfill our own needs, we are often afraid that our families and friends will suffer. However, the opposite is true. Just as a pebble thrown into a pond sends out ripples, those you love will be positively affected and supported as you grow and evolve. They will change as you change, even if they live far away from you, since all relationships are telepathic. Your growth and transformation will be reflected in others.

As I grow, everyone grows.

August 19

The dance of life

Female and male, being and doing, receiving and giving, destroying and creating, grieving and rejoicing — these polarities create the dance of life. Each of us contains within us the full spectrum of life's energies. To the degree that we accept and express all aspects of ourselves, we become whole and conscious channels of the universe.

I am experiencing and expressing the dance of life.

August 20

Be willing to follow that guidance

The nature of the feminine is wisdom, love, and clear vision expressed through feeling and desire. The masculine energy is all-out risk-taking action, in service to the feminine, much like the chivalrous knight and his lady. Remember now that we are talking about an internal process in each of us, male and female alike. We are not saying that men should let women tell them what to do, but that we each need to let our intuition guide us and then be willing to follow that guidance directly and fearlessly.

I am following the guidance of my intuition, directly and fearlessly.

August 21

Finding our wholeness

In the past men have desperately needed women to provide them with the nurturing, intuitive, and emotional support they need, and women have been dependent on men to take care of them and provide for them in the physical world. It seems like a perfect arrangement, except for one problem. When you don't feel whole, as an individual, when you feel your survival depends on others, you are constantly afraid of losing them.

We have been struggling with these "old male" and "old female" roles for many generations. So it is wonderful that we are beginning to discover that each of us has all the qualities within to be whole.

I am whole.

August 22

The male in women

Both the old male (macho) and the old female (submissive) exist in each sex. A woman who feels caught in the traditional female role has a controlling, macho old male inside of her, suppressing her. She will tend to attract men who mirror this male personality and will reflect it in their behavior toward her. This behavior may range from paternalistic and chauvinistic to verbally or physically abusive, depending on how the woman treats herself and what she believes she deserves. By acknowledging her own internal male, she takes the power of healing back into her own hands. As she begins to use her male energy to trust, support, and express her own inner feelings, her self-love will be reflected in her relationships.

My inner male loves and supports me.

August 23

The female in men

The traditional macho man has been taught to suppress and deny his inner female self, who becomes desperate to be recognized and loved. He will tend to attract women who have a low self-image, who are clinging and needy, or who express their power indirectly through manipulation, little girl cuteness, cattiness, or dishonesty. These women reflect his lack of trust and respect for his inner female by not trusting and respecting themselves. As he begins to recognize them as reflections of his own female, he can begin to love and honor the powerful, nurturing woman inside him.

*I trust and respect
my inner female.*

August 24

Men will reflect her shift

Once a woman begins to trust and love herself more, and starts to use her internal male energy to support herself, the behavior of men in her life will reflect that shift. They will either change dramatically and continue to change as she does, or they will disappear from her life to be replaced by men who are supportive and appreciative of her, mirroring her new attitude toward herself. I have seen this happen over and over again.

I support and appreciate myself.

August 25

Women will mirror his change

By opening to and trusting his own feminine nature, a man will find within himself the nurturing, support, and connection he has been lacking. The women in his life will mirror this shift by becoming stronger, more independent, more direct, honest, and more genuinely loving and nurturing.

As I nurture myself,
I am nurtured by others.

August 26

Ask for images of male and female

$\mathcal{G}$et in a comfortable position, close your eyes, relax your body. Now bring to your mind an image that represents your inner female. Take a look at your female and get a sense or a feeling of what she represents to you. Ask her if she has anything she would like to say to you and/or ask her any questions you may have. Once you have allowed yourself to receive her communication, take a deep breath and release her from your mind. Come back to a quiet, still place. Do the same process with the male. Then ask for the images of both male and female to come to you. See how they relate to one another. Ask them if they have anything they would like to communicate to each other or to you. Then once again take a deep breath and release these images from your mind. Come back to a still, quiet place.

I am in touch with my inner male and female.

August 27

When male and female are in harmony

I often imagine my male standing behind my female — supporting, protecting, backing her up. For a man the image might be reversed. You might see your female as within or behind you — guiding, empowering, nurturing, and supporting you. When male and female energies are in harmony and working together, it is an incredible feeling. One becomes a strong, open, creative channel with power, wisdom, peace, and love flowing through.

My male and female energies are working in harmony.

August 28

A mirror of yourself

If you know on a deep level that the person you are attracted to is a mirror of yourself, you know that everything that you see in your partner is also in you. The reason you are in relationships is to learn about yourself and deepen your connection with your higher self. Healthy relationships are based on the passion and excitement of sharing the journey of becoming a whole person.

I learn about myself through the mirror of my relationships.

August 29

A love affair with the universe

ecause many of us have never really learned how to take good care of ourselves, our relationships have been based on trying to get someone else to take care of us. In the past, we may have tried to use falling in love to fill up an empty space within us. We are now finding that being alive is a love affair with the universe. Life is a love affair between our inner male and female, between our form and our spirit.

I am now having a love affair with the universe.

August 30

Treat yourself the way you want to be treated

The qualities that women look for in men — strength, power, daring, excitement, romance — need to be developed within themselves. Likewise, men must develop the qualities they look for in women — caring, compassion, nurturing, tenderness, intuitiveness. Imagine how you'd want to be treated by a perfect lover, then begin to treat yourself exactly that way.

*I treat myself exactly the way
I want to be treated.*

August 31

Imagine the universe is your lover

Take yourself on a romantic date. Prepare for it as if you were going out with the most loving and exciting partner you can imagine. Take a luxurious hot bath. Dress up in your best clothes. Buy yourself flowers. Have a lovely dinner, or a moonlight stroll. Spend the evening telling yourself how wonderful you are, and anything else that you would like to hear from a lover. Imagine that the universe is your lover giving you everything you want.

The universe is my lover.

September 1

There are many selves within us

We are all born with an infinite number of different qualities or energies within us. One of our most important tasks in life is to discover and develop as many of these energies as possible, so that we can be well rounded, and experience the full range of our potential.

We can think of these energies as different archetypes, subpersonalities, or selves within us. In a way, it's as if there are many different characters living inside of us, each with its own task and purpose.

I am getting to know the many selves within me.

September 2

A fascinating movie

I am learning to view my life as a fascinating and adventurous movie. All the characters in it are reflections of parts of me played out on the big screen so that I can clearly see them. Once I see them and recognize their various feelings and voices inside myself, I can understand that they are all important and valuable parts of me that I need for my full expression in this life.

I appreciate and embrace the characters within me.

September 3

Everything wants to be loved

There is a simple universal principle: Everything in the universe wants to be accepted. All aspects of creation want to be loved, appreciated, and included. So, any quality or energy that you are not allowing yourself to experience or express will keep coming up inside of you or around you until you recognize it as a part of you, until you accept it and integrate it into your personality and your life.

I'm learning to love and accept all parts of me.

September 4

What is spiritual?

Many people who are involved in personal growth become very identified with the energies and qualities that they think of as being "spiritual" — peaceful, loving, giving, and so on. In attempting to develop these aspects of themselves, they often deny and disown other aspects that they consider to be "unspiritual" — aggression, assertiveness, gut-level honesty, human vulnerability. Unfortunately, this simply creates a huge shadow side within them, which contributes to the collective shadow of denied energies in our world.

I'm learning to honor all parts of myself, including the ones I've disowned.

September 5

Lovers are special mirrors

As we build and open our channel, more and more energy flows through, more feeling and passion. Certain people attract us very strongly and intensify or deepen our experience of the life force within us. These people are important mirrors for us and they are channels for special energy in our life. Through them we can learn some of the most important teachings life has to offer us.

My lover is my mirror.

September 6

A blissful moment

*F*alling in love is actually a powerful experience of feeling the universe move through you. The other person has become a catalyst that triggers you to open up to the love, beauty, and passion that is within you. Your channel opens wide and the universal energy comes pouring through. You have a blissful moment of fulfillment.

I am falling in love with life.

September 7

You receive what you always wanted

It is interesting that what we create within us is always mirrored outside of us. This is the law of the universe. When you have built an inner male and female who support and love you, there will always be men and women in your life reflecting this. When you truly give up trying to become whole through others, you end up receiving what you always wanted from others.

The more I love myself,
the more others love me.

September 8

Change old patterns

Take a good look at how external problems reflect your inner process. If you learn from your experiences and grow, your relationships will grow also.

A lot of these problems can be worked through by deeply and sincerely sharing your feelings, learning to take care of yourself, and by encouraging others to do the same. You may want to get support from a professional counselor or therapist to help you, or even your whole family, change old patterns.

*I am willing
to reach out for help.*

September 9

Find supportive therapy

It has been my experience that many of us need help in the form of supportive therapy or counseling to deal with deep levels of emotional healing. For some of us, there is a certain reluctance to seek help, perhaps because we fear it is an indication of weakness, sickness, or craziness. Personally, I have sought therapy of various types at many times in my life and it has helped me greatly as long as I trusted my own intuition about who to work with, when to stop, and so on. We give ourselves a great gift when we ask for help.

I have the courage to ask for help.

September 10

Be honest

If someone in your life — a friend, lover, or child is being secretive or dishonest with you, ask yourself if you have been really honest about your own feelings, with yourself or with them. Is there some way in which you don't trust yourself, and therefore don't trust them? If we are afraid to be real and honest, we don't feel safe in the world and we don't trust others. Our friends and family may reflect this attitude. As we reveal and express ourselves truthfully, we will attract honesty and openness from the world around us.

*I am honest
with myself and others.*

September 11

Children sense what you feel

If you are trying to appear calm and collected on the outside when actually you are feeling upset and angry, your children may mirror this to you by becoming wild and disruptive. While you are trying to maintain control, they pick up the chaotic energy inside of you and reflect it in their behavior. If you express directly what you are feeling, without trying to cover it up, they will usually calm down. They feel comfortable with the truth, the congruity between your feelings and your words. This is true of other relationships as well.

When I speak the truth,
people feel safe.

Our relationships are channels

$\mathcal{I}$ move toward people I love because I want the intensification I experience with them. I feel the universe moving through me to them and moving through them to me. This may happen by just being together, talking, or touching. The intuitive energy itself lets me know what is appropriate. It's mutually satisfying and fulfilling because the universe is giving to each through the channel of the other. If I trust my own energy, each person in the interaction receives what they need.

The universe is channeling
through my relationships.

September 13

Trust and appreciate your sexual energy

We are beginning to be more open and natural about our bodies and sexual energy. Because of our old conditioning, however, many of us still believe on a deep level that our sexual energy is a dangerous force. We distrust ourselves.

In fact our sexual energy comes from the same universal source as all other energy. It is the expression of that energy that confuses us. We either exaggerate it or shut it off, fearing that we won't get what we need or that we'll lose what we already have. Sexual energy itself is innocent. It is merely one way in which universal energy moves through us and draws us to the experiences we need for our learning, healing, and enjoyment.

I am willing to trust my sexual energy.

September 14

Feel and enjoy sexual energy

To be in a state of innocence about our sexuality, we first have to recognize how we deny or distort our feelings. For example, if you feel attracted to someone you meet at a party, do you notice yourself trying to manipulate them toward a sexual encounter? Or, do you find yourself suppressing the sexual feelings because you're afraid, or you're with someone else? In both cases you've blocked the enjoyment of the sexual feeling you are having, either by racing ahead with it, or by trying to ignore it. *It is okay to simply feel and enjoy our sexual energy.* We do not need to make anything happen. If it is appropriate for something more to happen, it will happen in a relaxed, natural way. And whether or not anything happens physically, we can still enjoy the feelings and the energy.

I enjoy feeling my sexual energy.

September 15

Trust your rhythm

People sometimes push beyond their natural sexual rhythm, either looking to satisfy needs unrelated to sex or rebelling against suppressive sexual rules. This pushing can eventually diminish their sexual energy. They seek increasingly stimulating ways to satisfy themselves, but satisfaction eludes them.

You can trust that your energy will bring you what you need. You can trust that your own rhythm is unique and beautiful. You can relax, enjoy, and listen to your own rhythm.

I respect my own sexual rhythm.

Allow yourself to feel

Many people are frightened of their sexual energy and have protected themselves by cutting it off and denying it. This kills the sexual energy and leaves them feeling frustrated, afraid of themselves and their passions. As you begin to recognize the universal source of this sexual energy, you can accept the feeling, knowing you do not have to "do" anything about it. You can just begin to allow yourself to feel and enjoy it.

It is safe for me
to feel sexual energy.

September 17

Honoring agreements

Following your energy does not mean acting out every impulse, feeling, or fantasy that you have — that would be the road to chaos. In order to follow your energy constructively, it's important to be aware of the various selves or voices within you, which may at times have conflicting feelings and needs. Through this kind of awareness, you can begin to sense the deeper intuitive feeling of where the life force is trying to take you, while honoring important agreements, boundaries, and commitments you may have with others.

While following my own energy,
I also honor the agreements and
commitments I have with others.

September 18

We are infinitely attractive

Many of us fear that we are not attractive or desirable enough to attract others. We have believed that we are "not enough." Today let's remind ourselves that we all receive our beauty, energy, and light from the same inexhaustible source. As we acknowledge this and begin to love and appreciate ourselves as we are, our channel opens and we have available to us the infinite vitality, beauty, and magnetism of the life force.

I am attractive, desirable, and lovable.

September 19

Receive appreciation

Imagine yourself in some everyday situation, and picture someone looking at you with great love and admiration, telling you something they really like about you. Now picture a few more people coming up and agreeing that you are a wonderful person. (Even if this embarrasses you, stick with it.) Imagine more and more people coming up. Picture yourself in a parade or on a stage and hear the applause ringing in your ears. Take a bow. Thank others for their support and appreciation.

I am a wonderful person.
I deserve love and appreciation.

September 20

Our bodies express our individual perfection

The body is continuously changing, replenishing, and rebuilding itself at every moment. The more we bring our consciousness into alignment with our highest spiritual aspiration, the more our bodies will express our own individual perfection.

My body expresses
my unique perfection.

September 21

Form a habit of being creative

Creative visualization is a basic and important tool in expanding our lives and creating our reality. Try creative visualization out in different situations and under different circumstances. If you find yourself worrying or puzzled about anything, or feeling weak, powerless, or frustrated about a situation, ask your intuitive guide whether there is a way you could use creative visualization to help you. Form a habit of being creative in every possible situation.

Each situation is an opportunity
to be creative.

September 22

Act as if it were true

By doing affirmations, you are replacing the old negative voices with new positive ones. When you first start using an affirmation, you may not believe it. In fact if you already believed it, there would be no need to affirm it. It is important, though, to try to tap into a *feeling* of belief and an experience that the affirmation *can* be true. Temporarily, at least for a few moments, suspend your doubts and hesitations and put your full mental and emotional energy into the affirmation. Act as if it were true.

*I am willing to believe
in myself.*

September 23

Messages from our bodies

One of the basic principles of holistic health is that we cannot separate our physical body from our emotional, mental, and spiritual states of being. For instance, when we have a physical disorder, it is a message for us to look deeply into our emotional and intuitive feelings, our thoughts and attitudes, to discover how we need to take better care of ourselves emotionally, mentally, or spiritually, as well as physically. With this approach, we can restore the natural harmony and balance within our being.

I am balanced and healthy.

September 24

Our stepping-stones to wholeness

In this new age, many of us have a tendency to deny any negative feelings. We judge them as "bad" or "unenlightened" when, in fact, they are our stepping-stones to wholeness. Our so-called negative feelings or attitudes are really parts of ourselves that need recognition, love, and healing. Not only is it safe and healthy to acknowledge and accept all our feelings and beliefs, it is necessary, if we are to get in touch with the fears and pockets of blocked energy that are holding us back from what we want.

In this wonderful new age, "enlightenment" means accepting ourselves as we are. Anything we no longer need will naturally be healed and released.

I accept myself as I am, and release what I no longer need.

September 25

Becoming aware of negative beliefs

Our negative thoughts are valuable messages to us about our deeper fears and negative attitudes. These usually are so basic to our thinking and feeling that we don't realize they are beliefs at all. We assume that they are simply "the way life is." We may be consciously affirming and visualizing prosperity, but if our unconscious belief is that we don't deserve it, then we won't create it. Once we become aware of our core negative beliefs, they begin to shift.

As I become aware of my negative beliefs, I heal them.

September 26

Healing negative beliefs

Here is a powerful method to discover and begin healing your unconscious negative beliefs. Sit silently and get in touch with a particular problem. Using a pencil and paper, describe the problem. Ask yourself these questions: 1) What emotions am I feeling? 2) What physical sensations am I feeling? 3) What old tapes or old programming am I running in my head? 4) What is the worst thing that could happen in this situation? 5) What is the best thing that could happen? 6) What fear or negative belief is keeping me from creating what I want in this situation? 7) Create an affirmation to counteract and heal the negative belief. For example, if the old belief is "I don't deserve to have what I want," the affirmation could be "I deserve to be happy."

I release old beliefs,
and create new, supportive ones.

September 27

We can reprogram our concepts

If we find that we are responding to our world in a way that is harmful or limiting, we can reprogram our old concepts and ideas about ourselves and about life. Because of the way the body and mind work together, and the constant mutual communication between them (the body registering information about the physical universe, transmitting it to the mind; the mind interpreting the meaning according to our experience and belief system, then sending appropriate messages back to the body), we are able to explore and release old beliefs that do not serve us. We can create, affirm, and visualize new beliefs that will serve us well.

My mind and my body work together
to serve my highest good.

September 28

A powerful and useful message

Sometimes we get sick because we believe on an unconscious level that illness is an appropriate or inevitable response to a situation or circumstance. In some way, it seems to solve a problem for us, give us something we need, or is a solution to an unresolved and unbearable inner conflict.

Rather than thinking of illness as disaster, we can think of it as a powerful and useful message. If we are suffering, it is a message that there is something to be looked at within our consciousness, something to be recognized, acknowledged, and healed. It may indicate that there is something about the way we are living that needs to be changed in order for us to be emotionally healthier.

*I am now listening
to what my body has to say.*

September 29

Healing on all levels

Sometimes, an illness may be a message from our bodies telling us that in some way we are not following our true energy or supporting our feelings. It starts with relatively subtle feelings of tiredness and discomfort. If we don't pay attention to these cues and make the appropriate changes, our bodies may give us stronger signals, including aches and pains. If we still don't change, sometimes more serious illness can occur. An illness may be a wake-up call that we need healing on an emotional and spiritual level as well as physically.

I listen to the messages my body gives me.

September 30

Imagine yourself in perfect health

Sit or lie down. Breathe and relax deeply. Imagine golden healing light energy all around your body. Feel it, sense it, enjoy it. Know you deserve this healing. Welcome it. Send this special, loving, healing energy to any part of you that needs it. See and feel it being healed. Picture the problem gently dissolving and flowing away. Imagine yourself in perfect health. Think of yourself in different situations feeling active, radiant, and healthy. Pick affirmations that work best for you and use them.

I am now in perfect health.

Fall

October 1

My primary relationship is with myself

*M*y primary relationship is my relationship with myself — all others are mirrors of it. As I learn to love myself, I automatically receive the love and appreciation that I desire from others. If I am committed to myself and to living my truth, I will attract others with equal commitment. My willingness to be intimate with my own deep feelings creates the space for intimacy with another.

As I learn to love myself, I receive
the love I desire from others.

October 2

Falling in love

Falling in love is the most thrilling and passionate experience in the world and of course we want to hold onto it. Because we recognize that another person has triggered this experience, we think it is he or she that is so wonderful. Actually, what we are experiencing is the love of the universe within ourselves.

I feel the love and passion of the universe within me.

October 3

You are seeing your own beauty

The next time that you feel romantic or sexual attraction to someone, stop right then and acknowledge that it is also your own beauty you are seeing. It is the universe that you are feeling. Keep reminding yourself that this is all part of your true love affair — with the universe, with life, with yourself.

I am always in love —
with the universe, with life, with myself.

October 4

True passion brings us together

rue passion brings us together, but fear often takes over shortly thereafter. The relationship may start to die almost as soon as it blooms. We panic and usually hold on even tighter. The initial experience of falling in love is so powerful, sometimes we spend years trying to re-create it. Often it's only when we give up and let go that the energy starts to flow again and we can touch that same feeling.

I let go and trust.

October 5

Visualize positive change

All too often in ongoing relationships we have gotten stuck in certain roles and images with each other which we find difficult to change. It's as if we've put ourselves and each other in certain boxes with labels on them. We find this very limiting and confining, but we don't know how to step out of it.

Begin to visualize and affirm new images for yourself and for the other person. See the potential for positive change within every person and every situation, and give energy and support to that positive change through creative visualization.

I imagine positive change in myself and in my relationships.

The potential for perfection

The potential for perfection lies in every relationship just as it lies within each individual. It's already there, we simply have to uncover it by dissolving all the layers of "stuff" we have put on top of it. Remember that perfection does not refer to some external model or standard, but rather the unique and changing perfection innate in every being and every connection between two beings.

*I am innately perfect
and so is everyone else.*

October 7

Give love to ourselves

When you are overly emotionally dependent on another person, life can become a constant state of fear. Because you depend on that person for your supply of love and protection, you must control that source at any cost, either directly, by using force, or indirectly, using various manipulations. Generally this happens subtly. "I'll give you what you need, so you will be just as dependent on me as I am on you. That way you will keep giving me what I need."

We can stop this endless circle by feeling the love we can give ourselves. We can connect with the true and inexhaustible source of love within and feel the power of the universe protecting us and filling our needs. As we learn to love ourselves in this way, we also draw to us love from others.

I love myself.

October 8

Seeing your own reflection

When a man is attracted to a woman, he can recognize her as a mirror of his feminine aspect. Through her reflection he can learn more about his own female side and move through whatever fears and barriers he may have to come to a deeper integration within himself. When a woman falls in love with a man, she is seeing her own male reflected in him. She can learn to strengthen and trust her masculine side.

I see my own reflection in others.

October 9

See desirable qualities in yourself

$\mathcal{G}$et in a comfortable position. Close your eyes. Relax your body. Bring to mind one person whom you admire or are attracted to. Ask yourself what qualities you find most attractive in that person. Do you see those same qualities in yourself? If not, try imagining that you possess them. Imagine how you would look, talk, and act. Picture yourself in a variety of situations and interactions. Continue to do this visualization regularly while you are developing these desired qualities.

> The qualities I admire in others,
> I have in myself.

October 10

Spiritual energy and sexual energy
are complementary

Many people still suffer from the mistaken idea that spiritual energy and sexual energy are opposing forces, instead of recognizing that they are the same force. People sometimes deny their sexuality in order to be more spiritual, creating a tremendous conflict within themselves, and eventually blocking the very energy they are seeking. Actually, spiritual energy and sexual energy are simply ways of expressing love for ourselves and others. Both are very powerful.

I honor my sexual energy
as a spiritual force.

October 11

The power to create and transform

Most of us have become masters at cutting off our sexual energy. We are afraid of ourselves and afraid of where our sexual energy will take us. We instinctively know that our sexual energy has the power to create and transform, and that there is nothing safe, stable, or sedentary about it. We are afraid of this, so instead of trusting our natural instincts, we learn to suppress them. As we become more comfortable with our own inner power, however, we allow the natural expression of our sexuality.

My sexual energy has the power to create and transform.

October 12

Sexual healing

Write down all your negative beliefs, thoughts, and fears about sex. When you have done that, close your eyes and see yourself turning your fears or negative beliefs over to your higher power. Take a deep breath and relax. When this exercise feels complete, write correlative affirmations to help you counteract the negative beliefs that you have listed. Use these affirmations regularly. If you have deep fears or blocks that don't seem to be healing, let your intuition guide you in finding a good therapist or support group to help you. Imagine yourself and your life free from these old beliefs and flowing with loving energy.

My life is unlimited and flowing with loving energy.

October 13

Feel without acting

Pretend for a day, an hour, or however long you want, that you have no preconceived ideas about what your sexual feelings are and what you should and should not do about them. Let yourself feel them without needing to act on them.

Enjoy the experience of feeling like a sensuous, sexual being without needing to prove or accomplish anything. Keep the focus on your own body and enjoy feeling the life force within you.

I feel the life force within me.

October 14

A place of innocence

As we free ourselves from our rules, limitations, and rebellions, we are able to discover our own natural sexual flow. We can then move to a place of innocence with our sexuality. We can feel our energy as pure, as the force of the universe moving through us. We can begin to trust and experience our sexual energy without the influence of preconceived ideas. This will free us to be spontaneous.

I am innocent and spontaneous.

Our lives are filled with sensuality

ooking at a flower or having a moment of eye contact with someone can be as pleasing and fulfilling as a physical sexual encounter. Our lives are filled with the sensuality of the universe. Certain experiences may allow us to feel it more intensely than others. As we open to our own sensuality, we experience more of the passion of life.

I feel the sensuality of the universe moment by moment.

October 16

Listening to ourselves

When we feel attracted to someone, we become afraid of their judgments or their expectations. We give our power away. Rather than trusting our intuition and expressing ourselves directly, we often put our trust in a set of rules about how we should behave. We become anxious, thinking, "If I say this, he or she won't like it." Try saying exactly what you mean. Allow yourself to do what you want in the moment, not what you think others expect. Be honest with yourself. In this way we can learn to trust ourselves and to find true intimacy with others.

I trust myself.

Explore without expectation

Knowing that you will support your feelings in any given moment gives you the freedom and safety to explore your sexual energy without the expectation that it must be done "right." There are fears, excitement, and uncertainty surrounding sex as we start to explore our energy. All these feelings come to the surface to be healed. We can accept all of them without criticizing ourselves. The more we become able to accept these feelings, the gentler the process of exploration.

All of my feelings
are valid.

October 18

Express your feelings

If you want to make love and your partner doesn't, or vice versa, support and express the feelings you have. Then try to really listen to your partner's feelings. If possible, see if both of you can go under the surface and look for the deeper feelings involved.

It may be that you and your partner need to talk about some unexpressed hurt or anger. Or one of you may need some time alone. Keep supporting and expressing what you feel, so the energy may move freely.

It is safe for me to support and express my sexual feelings.

October 19

A different form of sensuality

Be open to expressing a different form of sensuality than usual. This energy may lead you and your partner into simply sitting together, lying together, holding each other, massaging one another, dancing, or something else you don't ordinarily think of as sex, but which can be just as satisfying. Be true to your feelings and the right actions will emerge.

If you don't have a partner at this time, be creative in finding ways to express your sensuality individually or with a friend through dancing, massage, being in nature, or whatever inspires you.

I express my love and sensuality in many ways.

October 20

Merging and separating

All beings have a deep yearning to merge with another being. When we feel mutual love and attraction with another person, we allow ourselves to merge energetically with them and experience that feeling of bliss. Then we need to separate again in order to reestablish our sense of our own identity. This is sometimes difficult, as we tend to hold on to that merged state, fearing that if we lose it we'll never find it again and we'll feel too alone. So we stay semi-merged and eventually feel resentful because we feel we have no personal space of our own. Sometimes we fight in order to create separation. We need to learn to separate cleanly and honestly by establishing our boundaries and taking the space we need. A good relationship is a constant dance of merging and separation.

I merge deeply and blissfully; I separate and take my own space clearly and easily.

October 21

The keys to intimacy

A relationship becomes stagnant when people are no longer willing to tell each other how they really feel. When people first fall in love, they are eager to communicate their feelings because they are still getting to know each other and dependency has not yet set in. As soon as it does, people often stop sharing their true feelings, or they begin to manipulate, fearing they might lose the relationship. To keep a relationship as fresh and alive as it was in the beginning, keep sharing your feelings directly even though it may be a little frightening to do so. Vulnerability and honesty are the keys to intimacy.

I share my feelings honestly with those I love.

October 22

Be true to yourself

Passion disappears when we are no longer open to our feelings, when we sacrifice being true to ourselves in order to hold on to someone else. To experience passion, we must first be true to ourselves and then honest with others.

Passion in a partnership comes from true intimacy with each other. As we become an open channel for our feelings, we become an open channel for the passion and joy that can flow through us.

I am true to myself and honest with others.

October 23

Clear communication

I've found a very interesting thing. When I communicate truthfully and directly, in a nonblaming, nonjudgmental way, and say everything I really want to say, it doesn't seem to matter so much how the other person responds. They may not do exactly what I want, but I feel so clear and empowered from taking care of myself that it's easier to let go of the result. If I keep being honest and vulnerable with my feelings to my partner, family, and friend, I won't end up with hidden needs or resentments.

I'm learning to communicate honestly without blame and judgment.

October 24

Ask for what you need, then let go

When you take care of yourself by asking clearly and directly for what you need, more often than not you do get what you ask for. If not, the next step is to let go. Go inside yourself and tune in to what your intuition is telling you to do next. Always let it take you to a deeper connection with yourself and the universe.

I ask for what I need and let go of the results.

October 25

The relationship will unfold

We must be willing to let our relationships reveal themselves to us. If we are true to ourselves, expressing ourselves fully and honestly, the relationship will unfold in its own unique and fascinating way. You never know exactly where it will lead. It keeps changing its mood, flavor, and form from minute to minute, day to day, and year to year. At times it may take you closer to each other, at times it may take you further apart, but each stage in the relationship can be an adventure when we are trusting the universe.

My relationships are unfolding in unique and special ways.

October 26

There is something to learn

People often wonder what to do when they are involved in a monogamous relationship and find themselves attracted to someone else. Usually when we block the energy and deny the attraction, we find that it becomes a bigger problem. It's best to be honest with ourselves and our partner about the feelings. We need to look deeper within ourselves to see what it is that we are most attracted to in this other person. Perhaps it is a quality that is underdeveloped in ourselves and/or our primary relationship. The situation can strengthen our primary relationship if we are willing to learn from it and if we act with integrity. If necessary, get a facilitator to help.

*I'm willing to learn and grow
from every experience.*

October 27

Keep telling the truth

When I am willing to be honest, ask for what I want, and share my feelings openly, I always find that the underlying truth in any situation is the same for all concerned. At first it may seem that I want one thing and the other person wants something else. If we both keep telling the truth as we feel it, sooner or later we will discover that we both can have what we truly want. We can trust that the universe wants us to be happy and fulfilled. We tell ourselves the truth; we tell each other the truth. This is love.

The universe wants me to be happy and fulfilled.

October 28

I commit to myself

Whether or not I am in a primary partnership at this time, I am always in a relationship with myself! It is important to make a commitment to myself — to love, honor, obey, and cherish my own being. To anyone I love, I promise to do the best I can to tell the truth, to share my feelings, to take responsibility for myself, to honor the connection I feel with that person, and to maintain that connection.

I am committed to myself.

October 29

Allow the form to change

When we don't know how to allow the form of a relationship to change while still honoring the underlying love and connection, it causes pain in that relationship. When you are deeply involved with another being, that connection lasts forever. After you have learned a great deal from being with someone, the energy between you may eventually diminish to the point where you no longer need to interact on a personality level as much, or at all. Yet, the connection between your two spirits remains strong. Sometimes the energy renews itself again on another level.

*It is natural and safe
for my relationships to change form.*

October 30

Communicating honestly can help

Changes in a relationship sometimes leave us feeling guilty, disappointed, and hurt. We don't know how to share our feelings effectively, so we respond by cutting off our connection with the other person. This causes real pain, because we are cutting off our own deep feelings. Changes can be less painful and even beautiful when we communicate honestly and trust ourselves in the process.

I approach change with honesty and trust in myself.

October 31

Every being is free to choose who to love

For some people, being in a close, intense relationship with a person or persons of the same sex is the most powerful mirroring process they can find. I think many of these things are mysteries that we will understand only in retrospect, but I believe that every being chooses the life path and relationships that will help him or her to grow the fastest.

I do have a strong sense that on a spiritual level homosexual and bisexual relationships are a powerful step that some beings take to break through old rigid roles and stereotypes to find their own truth. The core purpose in every relationship is for each of us to grow and evolve.

I accept and honor each person's right to choose.

November 1

An ongoing masterwork

The physical world is our creation: we each create our own version of the world, our particular reality, our unique life experience. Because I am creating my life, I can look at my creation to get feedback about myself. Just as an artist looks at his latest creation to see what works well and what doesn't, and thereby improves his skills, we can look at the ongoing masterwork of our lives to appreciate who we are and to recognize what we still need to learn.

My life is my creation.

November 2

No accidents

$\mathcal{I}$ assume that *everything* in my life is my reflection, my creation; there are no accidents or events that are unrelated to me. If I see or feel something, if it has any impact on me, then my soul has attracted or created it to show me something. If it didn't mirror some part of myself, I wouldn't even be able to see it. All the people in my life are reflections of the various characters and energies that live inside of me.

Everything in my life
is my reflection.

November 3

Everything is a gift

I always try to avoid putting myself down for the reflections I see. I know that nothing is negative. Everything is a gift that brings me to self-awareness — after all, I'm here to learn. If I was already perfect, I wouldn't be here. Why should I get angry at myself when I see things I've been unconscious of? It would be like a first grader getting frustrated because she wasn't in college yet. I try to maintain a compassionate attitude toward myself and my learning process. To the extent that I can do this, the learning process becomes fun and really quite interesting.

I'm here to learn.

November 4

Our primary creation

Our body is our primary creation, the vehicle we have chosen to express us in the physical world. By looking at our bodies, listening to them, and feeling them, we can read a great deal about our spiritual, mental, and emotional energy patterns. The body is our primary feedback mechanism that can show us what is and isn't working about our way of thinking, expressing, and living.

I'm learning from my body.

November 5

Trust your body

Having a beautiful body starts with following the natural flow of your energy. We have been taught to distrust our bodies and see them as needing to be controlled. Trust yourself. Sleep as much as you want. Stay in bed if you need more rest. Express yourself physically in ways that feel good. Eat what your body desires and follow your heart. If you are willing to trust your body, you'll learn what's best for you.

I trust my body.

Beliefs about our bodies

*M*ost of us have negative beliefs about our bodies and/or the foods we eat. It is important to examine these beliefs and become more conscious of what we tell ourselves. Write down all your beliefs about food and/or your body. Write down anything that comes to you, even if it doesn't make sense or seem connected. Keep writing, the more the better. In making these beliefs more tangible, we are taking a most important step in our healing.

*It is safe for me
to look at my negative beliefs.*

November 7

Origin of beliefs

Examine your present beliefs about your body. Try to remember where you first learned some of them. Did you pick them up from a parent, sibling, teacher, or a friend? Don't struggle to establish the origin of all your beliefs. Simply look at the ones that affect you most deeply, and observe the connections and memories that surface. Feel the feelings associated with these memories and consciously let them go.

It is an act of courage and self-love to look at the origins of your beliefs, to consciously feel and release them. The end result is a new sense of freedom and lightness.

I feel lighter and freer.

November 8

Time to let go

When you have identified beliefs about your body that no longer serve you, it's time to let go of them. Realize they have served you for years. Thank them for the service they have provided and let them know you are willing to let go of them. Feel the release and freedom of being who you are now.

As I let go of the old way, a new way is shown to me.

Focus on what you like

Too often we focus on what needs to be changed about ourselves. We are waiting for perfection before we'll love ourselves completely. You can change this self-critical programming by looking at what you like about yourself and giving yourself positive feedback. Appreciate the beauty in your body and focus on the qualities you admire in yourself. Your body will respond to this appreciation and grow increasingly beautiful.

I see many things
I like about myself.

November 10

Thank your body

lie down in a comfortable position and close your eyes. Imagine there is healing energy coming through your hands, and put your hands on whatever part of your body seems to want your attention. Send healing and love to that area. Then move your hands to another area. Find a way to appreciate every part of yourself and thank your body for being with you for all these years, following your desires and serving you. If you like, you can play music that you love and use candles or flowers while performing this ritual.

My body is my friend.

Beauty treatments

Do things for yourself regularly that make you feel you are taking special care of yourself and doing nice things for your body.

Take a hot bath or shower and visualize the hot water totally relaxing, soothing, and healing you. Picture any problems melting or being washed away, and nothing remaining but your natural radiance shining from within.

Put lotion on your face and body, giving yourself lots of loving attention, affirming that your skin is becoming smoother and more beautiful all the time.

I regularly do nice things for my body.

Eating ritual

Sit down with your food in front of you. Close your eyes, relax, and take a deep breath. Silently thank the universe for this food and thank all the beings who helped provide it, including the plants and animals, the people who grew it and prepared it for you.

Open your eyes and look at the food; really observe how it looks and smells. Slowly begin to eat, thoroughly enjoying the taste. Tell yourself that this food is being transformed into life energy for your use. Picture yourself becoming healthier and more beautiful as a result of eating this food.

Take a moment after you finish to enjoy the pleasant, warm glow that emanates from your stomach when it is satisfied and happy.

I enjoy my food.

Physical exercise

No matter what type of physical exercise you do, you can use creative visualization and affirmation to help you get maximum benefit and enjoyment from it.

For example, if you like to run, picture yourself running very swiftly, smoothly, and tirelessly. If you dance or do yoga, put your awareness in your body, in your muscles; picture them relaxing and stretching; see yourself becoming more and more accomplished until you are truly excelling.

*I love exercising my body.
I am strong, limber, and physically fit.*

The universe is the true parent
of your children

The universe is the true parent of your children. You are simply the channel. The more you are able to follow your energy and do what is best for you, the more the universe will come through you to everyone around you. As you thrive, your children thrive.

The universe is taking care of me
and my loved ones.

November 15

Parents need to continue to grow

For many parents, having children has been a convenient excuse for abandoning their own growth. They spend most of their time focusing on the children, making sure that they learn and grow properly. But in taking responsibility for the lives of their children, parents often abandon responsibility for their own, forgetting that children will respond positively when we choose to live our lives for our own greatest growth.

I take responsibility for my own growth.

Sense the powerful being within

This is the day for recognizing the true beauty, power, and magic within each other and in ourselves. Get comfortable. Close your eyes, relax, and take a few deep breaths. Picture or imagine your child or someone that you love in front of you. Look into their eyes and sense the powerful being within them. Take enough time to receive feelings, ideas, or impressions about who this being really is. Communicate to them your respect and appreciation. Imagine that this person is communicating respect and appreciation to you.

I respect myself and my loved ones as powerful human beings.

We all have healing power

A part of our consciousness is directly linked with everyone else's consciousness. Since this is also our link with the divine omnipotence and omniscience, it means that we all have incredible healing power which we can tap into at will. If even one of us possesses the power to heal, in fact, we all possess the power to heal, and all of us receive that power from the same magnificent source.

*I have the power
to heal.*

Healing meditation

Relax deeply. Think of yourself as a clear channel through which the healing energy of the universe is pouring. As clearly as you can, picture or think of someone who wants to be healed and ask him what he would like you to do for him in your meditation. See any problems in his body, mind, or heart dissolved, and see everything being healed and functioning perfectly. Surround him with golden healing light. See him radiant, healthy, and happy. Remind him that he is a perfect being. When you feel the meditation is complete, open your eyes.

I am a clear channel for the healing energy of the universe.

November 19

Trusting our natural flow

We are taught at an early age that expressing ourselves and fulfilling our needs naturally is not socially acceptable. Therefore, we learned how to suppress many of our natural desires, causing conflict and imbalance in our system and rebellion in our body and spirit. Often we react by going for the quickest available "high." Our bodies react to this imbalance by gaining weight, losing weight, becoming tense, or developing allergies and addictions. We crave all kinds of things we would not normally desire if left to our own natural flow.

We now have the tools to reconnect with our natural desires, honor the voice of our spirit, the voice of our intuition, which tells us what is best for us.

I follow the flow of my natural desires.

November 20

Become willing to receive help

Realize that we all use some form of addiction to pace ourselves, to keep ourselves from experiencing our feelings and our power. The cure for this is to build a trust in ourselves and the universe. We need to become increasingly willing to experience our vulnerable feelings as well as our strength. For those who have a drug, food, or alcohol addiction, the physical craving overrides any awareness. The body and the drug are blocking any voice of the spirit. Help and support are needed. A professional substance abuse counselor or a group such as Alcoholics, Narcotics, or Overeaters Anonymous can help one abstain from drug and food abuse. This gives the body a chance to heal and the spirit a chance to be heard.

*I am willing to
receive help from others.*

November 21

Addiction is control

The more uncomfortable we are about trusting our natural energy, the more likely we are to display addictive behavior such as exccssive use of coffee, alcohol, unwholesome foods, drugs, over-work, and dependent relationships. Many people are afraid of being "too much" or "too little." Addiction becomes a means to pace, or suppress our power.

As we develop a trust in the universe, we are no longer overwhelmed by our own power and creativity. We are learning that surrender to this higher power is the path of healing. We can experience the ecstasy of being at one with the natural flow of the universe.

I trust my natural energy.

November 22

Assertion is vital

When we are afraid to be assertive, to express our true feelings, we may find ourselves using substances as a means of either voicing these feelings or suppressing them. The process of assertion is vital. As we back our feelings with action, we create an internal strength and protection. We feel safe moving into new situations, knowing that we will be able to say "no" to anything that doesn't feel good to us and "yes" to what does. We know that we will be true to ourselves and take good care of ourselves.

It is safe for me to assert my true feelings.

November 23

An epidemic of workaholism

Our culture is obsessed with achievement and productivity. As a result we have an epidemic of workaholism in which most of us push ourselves much harder than is necessary or healthy. We need to learn to relax, nurture ourselves, and balance work with pleasure and fun.

I give myself permission to relax and enjoy myself.

November 24

Make a contribution to the world

People often wonder what they are going to be when they grow up. What is it that they are going to do? What is their true purpose? Each of us has a true purpose and each one of us is a channel for the universe. When we follow our inner truth, life is creative and transformational. We make a contribution to the world just by being ourselves in every moment.

I make a contribution just by being myself.

Work and play can be the same

When you are following your energy and doing what feels right to you, moment by moment, the distinction between work and play tends to dissolve. Work is no longer what you *have* to do, and play what you *want* to do. When you are doing what you love, you may work harder and produce more than ever before, but you will experience such pleasure and enjoyment in your work that at times it may feel like play.

I enjoy my work.

November 26

The greatest reward

There need not be rigid categories in our lives — this is work, this is play. Let it all blend into the flow of following the guidance of the universe, and money will flow in as a result of the open channel that is created. You will no longer work just to make money or in order to sustain life. The delight that comes from expressing yourself becomes the greatest reward. The money comes as a natural part of this process.

As I express myself,
money flows through my channel.

November 27

Working and receiving money

For some, working and receiving money may no longer be directly related to each other. You are doing what you want to do and money is coming into your life. It is no longer a matter of doing work and then getting paid for it. The two things may be operating simultaneously in your life, but not necessarily in a direct cause and effect relationship.

I follow my energy and the universe takes care of me.

November 28

Gratitude

On our path of self-development, we often examine our growth with an eye to what we have yet to achieve. It is very important, however, to become aware of what we have already accomplished.

Make a gratitude list. Write down the ways in which you have changed, and the gifts you have allowed into your life. Acknowledge yourself for your dedication to personal growth. Consider how your family and friends have helped to bring you to this place on your path. Include those people who have served as great mirrors and teachers in your healing.

Close your eyes. Sense and visualize all the wondrous things that have happened, all the gifts you now have in your life, and give thanks for each of them with the whole of your heart.

I am grateful!

Attunement to your higher purpose

This is a good time to take a look at your past visualizations and notice how many of them have already manifested in your life. As you continue to express your gratitude for these, your ability to use creative visualization will expand and become a powerful force for creation. You will find that you become more and more attuned to and aware of your higher purpose.

Notice the elements that tend to recur in your dreams, goals, and fantasies and the particular qualities of the things you find yourself doing and creating. These are important clues to the underlying meaning and purpose of your life.

*I am in touch
with the purpose of my life.*

Acknowledge our higher purpose

We all know in our hearts what our higher purpose is, but we do not often consciously acknowledge it. In fact, many of us seem to go to great
lengths to hide it from ourselves and the world. We
fear the power, responsibility, and light that comes
with acknowledging and expressing our true purpose in life. Often we are afraid that our higher
purpose means giving up everything that brings us
comfort and love. In fact, our higher purpose and
our greatest joy are always in perfect alignment.

*I know and express
my higher purpose.*

One big learning experience

Life is always attempting to move us in the direction of our own evolution and development. This takes place in many different ways. In fact, every experience and event of our lives is part of that process. Most people are relatively unaware of this fact. They are passive participants in their evolutionary journey, or even actively resist it, if life isn't going the way they feel it should. Once we become aware of the fact that life is one big learning experience, it's easier to cooperate with the process. We can actively support and participate in our own healing and growth.

I welcome every experience as part of my evolution.

December 2

Choose your teachers well

Fortunately we live in a time when there are many tools, techniques, teachers, guides, and mentors to help us along the way. It is important to choose carefully who we allow to influence us. Remember that everyone has their human flaws and limitations, even the most seemingly evolved or enlightened.

We can learn much and receive considerable support from others, as long as we don't give our power away to anyone else. It is essential to keep the ultimate authority within ourselves.

I can learn from others while trusting my own sense of what's right for me.

December 3

Move into the world

Our eastern and western spiritual traditions have involved some degree of renunciation of the world. Relationships, money, material possessions, pleasures, and luxuries have been seen as temptations that draw us away from our spiritual development.

Those of us who choose to be spiritual seekers and transformers must now move *into* the world *with the same degree of commitment* to our spiritual selves as we would have if we renounced the world. This path is much more difficult!

I stay deeply connected to myself as I live fully in the world.

Embrace life

We are now challenged to surrender to the universe, to follow its guidance and to do so *while* having deep, passionate relationships, dealing with money, business, family, creative projects, and so many other "worldly" things. Rather than avoiding our attachments to the world, the time has come to acknowledge and work with them. We must move *into* the challenging situation, move into, recognize, and own all the feelings and attachment, and learn to embrace the full range of our experience.

I embrace all aspects of life.

December 5

We are in charge of our own journey

When someone dies, they are consciously or unconsciously choosing to leave this physical body. On the physical plane, it may appear that they are victims of disaster or deadly disease, but spiritually, they are in charge of their own journey. Their soul knows what it is doing even if their personality does not. When you start to believe this, you will also feel it telepathically and it will ease the pain of your loss. It is possible to grieve while knowing that the higher self of your loved one has chosen this path at this time, just as you also will choose your path and your time.

I am in charge of my own journey.

December 6

Changing our deepest attitudes

earning to use creative visualization can become a process of deep and meaningful growth. We often discover ways in which we have been holding ourselves back, allowing our fears and negative concepts to block ourselves from achieving satisfaction and fulfillment in life. The process of change that occurs does not occur on a superficial level, through mere positive thinking. It involves exploring, discovering, and changing our deepest, most basic attitudes toward life.

I am exploring, discovering, and changing.

December 7

Face your fears

If you have a lot of heavy emotions riding on whether you attain a goal, you may tend to work against yourself. In that case, it may be most effective and appropriate to work first on your feelings about the matter. You may have to take a good look at what you fear about achieving or not achieving your goal. Affirmations and clearing processes can help you feel more confident and secure.

Once you acknowledge the emotions and fears you have about your desire, you come to a place of greater peace with yourself. Paradoxically, this often clears the way for the original goal to be realized.

I am facing my fears.

December 8

Be flexible

$\mathcal{G}$oing with the flow means keeping your destination clearly in mind and yet enjoying all the beautiful scenes you encounter along the way. If life starts taking you in another direction, be willing to change your destination. Be flexible. Savor all the surprises life brings, and life in turn will bring more and more wonderful surprises to you.

I am ready for life's surprises.

December 9

Everything is unfolding perfectly

You will find in using creative visualization that your ability to manifest will work to the degree that you are in alignment with your higher purpose. If you try to manifest something and it doesn't seem to work, it may not be appropriate to the underlying pattern and meaning of your life. Be patient and keep tuning into your inner guidance. In retrospect you will see that everything is unfolding perfectly.

*Everything is
unfolding perfectly.*

December 10

Follow your intuitive feelings

Notice what happens when you doubt, suppress, or act contrary to your feelings. You will observe decreased energy, powerless or helpless feelings, and physical or emotional pain. Now notice what happens when you follow your intuitive feelings. Usually the result is increased energy and power and a sense of natural flow. When you're at one with yourself, the world feels peaceful, exciting, and magical.

I am following my intuition and my life is fulfilling.

December 11

Listen to the message

If you are feeling tired or ill, rest. Your body will always want rest and ease if it's sick. When you become quiet, ask your body what you need to do in order to heal yourself. Your body may tell you to change certain habits, to eat more wholesome food, or to express some feelings. It may tell you to quit your job or to see a doctor. It may have some other message for you, but there is always an answer available to you. The key is to ask and then listen honestly for a response.

I listen to my body.

December 12

Earth is our collective body

If you are concerned about environmental issues, consider this: Mother Nature is symbolic of the nurturing feminine aspect of ourselves. Disrespect and lack of harmony with nature are only possible in a society of individuals who disrespect and disregard their own feminine intuitive nature. If you are attuned to your inner guidance, there is no way you can become severely out of balance with your natural environment. In a sense, earth is our collective body. The way we treat her mirrors the way we treat our own bodies.

I am in harmony with my body and the earth.

December 13

Loving our earth

The lack of respect and attunement to our bodies is demonstrated on a global level by the way we treat the body of our planet. As we learn to trust and love our bodies, listen to their signals, give them food, rest, and nurturing, stop polluting them with drugs and unwholesome food, stop trying to control them with our artificial rules and ideas, I believe we will be able to treat our earth body with the same care and respect.

As I nurture my body,
I nurture the earth.

December 14

Abundance is our natural state

There is more than enough to go around for every being on earth if we are willing to open our minds to the possibility. We are not yet experiencing our world as rich and abundant because we have not fully opened to the true nature of the universe. We believe in the inevitability of poverty and scarcity and do not yet realize that the ultimate power of creation rests in the hands, minds, and hearts of each of us.

I am opening to the true abundance of life.

December 15

Appreciate the earth

Picture yourself in a lovely, natural environment. Take time to imagine all the beautiful details. Begin to wander and explore, finding more and more exquisitely beautiful environments of great variety — mountains, forests, deserts, oceans. Appreciate this magnificent earth on which we live. Imagine a world full of people living simply yet abundantly, in harmony with one another and the earth.

I am learning to live in harmony with the earth.

December 16

As we change, our world changes

Because the external world is truly our mirror, as we change, it must change. You can see this easily in your personal life. As you develop the habit of trusting and taking care of yourself, you will gradually release your old patterns. Soon you may notice that your friends, family, and other people around you seem to be acting differently, reflecting this change as well.

The world is my mirror.

*Individual change affects
the collective consciousness*

$\mathcal{E}$very individual's consciousness is a part of the collective consciousness. When a small but significant number of individuals have moved into a new level of awareness and truly changed their beliefs and their behavior, the change is felt in the entire collective consciousness. Every other individual is then moved in the direction of that change. The whole process may have started with one individual making the first leap.

As I transform,
the world is transformed.

December 18

Transformation spreads rapidly

Transformation begins with an individual and moves out into the world. The more you trust your intuition and act on it, experience and accept your feelings, the more the energy of the universe can move through you. Everyone around you will benefit from your energy. It heals and transforms them. In turn, they become more powerful channels for everyone in their sphere of influence, thus transformation spreads rapidly throughout the world.

My energy heals and transforms others.

December 19

The world is our reflection

Some believe that in order to change the world, all we have to do is think more positively about it and visualize the change we desire. Visualization and affirmation are powerful tools, to be sure, but there is more to it than that.

If the world is our mirror, then whatever we see out there in some way reflects what is in us. We need to take responsibility for it and be willing to transform it within ourselves if we want to see change in the world.

I take responsibility for my outer world by taking responsibility for my inner world.

December 20

Healing ourselves and the world

Notice the social, political, and environmental issues around you that trigger the most emotional reaction in you. Ask how they may reflect your personal issues, fears, beliefs, and patterns.

Ask for the higher power of the universe to release and heal the ignorance, fear, and limitation within you and in the world. Regularly visualize your life and the world as you would like them to be. Ask your inner guidance to let you know clearly if there is any specific action you need to take toward your own or the world's healing. Then continue to trust and follow your intuition.

The higher power of the universe is healing me and the world.

December 21

Shine light in the darkness

When we are willing to recognize and heal any form of violence, poverty, and imbalance within ourselves as individuals, we begin to eradicate these problems from our world.

Healing does not take place on a personal or planetary level if we hide or deny our feelings. Our feelings, beliefs, and emotional patterns must be brought to the light of consciousness in order to be transformed. When light shines in the darkness, the darkness disappears.

I accept and embrace my darkness and my light.

December 22

We are all cocreators

Do not take the blame or feel guilty for the world's problems. None of us is truly responsible for the lives of others. We are all cocreating this world together, and we are all doing it with limited knowledge. We are here to learn and we learn from what is imperfect rather than blaming ourselves for those imperfections.

We can adopt a positive attitude of responsibility by saying, "I am willing to learn to trust and follow my own inner truth, knowing that as I do, I will release the pain and fear within me, and thus help to heal the pain and fear in the world."

As I heal myself,
I help to heal the world.

Doing what you love

If you are trusting your intuition and following your heart, going where your energy takes you, and doing what you really want to do, you will see that your actions have a positive effect in changing the world. For many, this will include direct social and political action. People around you will be affected by your energy and vitality, even more than they are affected by your words and actions.

*I am now doing
what I love.*

The spirit of giving

This morning take a few minutes to reflect on how you give of yourself to the world. Often we get caught up in the frenzy of buying and giving *things.*

Look at the ways you give appreciation, friendship, energy, time, love, and affection, and give your own special talents and abilities throughout the year. Acknowledge yourself for having enriched the lives of others. Spend some time loving yourself for the giving light that you are.

I honor myself
for all that I give.

December 25

Your own divinity

In the stillness of meditation be with your own divinity. Pause and quietly rejoice in the feeling of oneness with the universe. At some point in your life's path you became aware that there is more to life than what you perceive with your physical senses alone. At that moment your own spirituality was born in you.

*I celebrate the birth
of my spirituality.*

December 26

What you create comes back

Whatever you try to create for another will always come back to you. That includes both loving, helpful, or healing actions and negative, destructive ones. This means, of course, that the more you use creative visualization to love and serve others as well as your own highest good, the more love, happiness, and success will find their way to you.

I create the highest good for myself and others.

December 27

The universe comes through many channels

When we feel an attraction to someone, it may be as brief as a glance or a short conversation with a stranger. It may be an ongoing contact — a profound relationship that lasts for many years. Either way, we are experiencing the universe at work. In these encounters, we can see the universe coming to us constantly through many different channels.

I see the universe
in everyone I encounter.

Trust the process of change

Real commitment makes no guarantees about a relationship's form. It allows for the fact that form is constantly changing, and that we can trust the process of change. It opens the door to true intimacy, created when people share deeply and honestly with one another. If two people stay together on this basis, they really want to be together. They continue to find an intensity of love and learning with each other as they change and grow.

I am willing to trust
the process of change.

December 29

Your life is your work of art

I like to think of myself as an artist, and my life is my greatest work of art. Every moment is a moment of creation, and each moment of creation contains infinite possibilities. I can do things the way I've always done them, or I can look at all the different alternatives, and try something new and different and potentially more rewarding. Every moment presents a new opportunity and a new decision.

What a wonderful game we are all playing, and what a magnificent art form....

My life
is a work of art.

December 30

A magical new city

I see an ancient city, gray and decaying. It is literally disintegrating, the old structures crumbling into piles of rubble. But it is being pushed aside, because in its place a beautiful, new city is arising. This new city is magical — it seems to shimmer delicately with every color of the universe. I know that it is being built inside of us. It is created from the light.

The light within me is creating miracles in my life here and now.

December 31

Envision the future

Imagine your personal future as you would like it to on all levels — spiritual, mental, emotional, and physical.

Now expand your focus to imagine the future of the world around you — your community, your country, humanity, the natural environment, our planet. Allow them all to reflect the integration and wholeness you have found within yourself. Imagine the new world emerging and developing in a healthy, balanced, expansive way.

I envision a wonderful future
for myself and the world.

Recommended Resources

Books

Allen, Marc. *A Visionary Life.* New World Library, 1998.

Gawain, Shakti. *Creative Visualization,* 25th Anniversary Edition. Nataraj/New World Library, 2002.

Gawain, Shakti. *Living in the Light,* Revised Edition. Nataraj/New World Library, 1986, 1998.

Gawain, Shakti. *The Path of Transformation: How Healing Ourselves Can Change the World,* Revised Edition. Nataraj/New World Library, 1993, 2000.

Gawain, Shakti. *The Four Levels of Healing: A Guide to Balancing the Spiritual, Mental, Emotional, and Physical Aspects of Life.* Nataraj/New World Library, 1997.

Gawain, Shakti. *Creating True Prosperity.* Nataraj/New World Library, 1997.

Stone, Hal and Sidra. *Embracing Our Selves: The Voice Dialogue Manual.* Nataraj/New World Library, 1993.

Stone, Hal and Sidra. *Embracing Each Other: Relationship as Teacher, Healer, and Guide.* Nataraj/New World Library, 1993.

Stone, Hal and Sidra. *Partnering.* Nataraj/New World Library, 1999.

Audios

Gawain, Shakti. *Living in the Light: Book on Tape.* Revised Edition. Nataraj/New World Library, 1998.

Gawain, Shakti. *Creative Visualization: Book on Tape.* Revised Edition. Nataraj/New World Library, 1995.

Gawain, Shakti. *Creative Visualization Meditations.*
Nataraj/New World Library, 1996.

Gawain, Shakti. *The Path of Transformation: Book on Tape.*
Abridged version. Nataraj/New World Library, 1993.

Gawain, Shakti. *The Four Levels of Healing: A Guide to
Balancing the Spiritual, Mental, Emotional, and Physical
Aspects of Life.* Nataraj/New World Library, 1997.

Gawain, Shakti. *Creating True Prosperity: Book on Tape.*
Nataraj/New World Library, 1997.

Stone, Hal and Sidra. *Meeting Your Selves.* Delos, 1990.

Video Tapes

Gawain, Shakti. *The Creative Visualization Workshop Video.*
Nataraj/New World Library, 1999.

Index